THE COMPLETE
CARIBBEAN COOKBOOK

THE COMPLETE
CARIBBEAN
COOKBOOK

TOTALLY TROPICAL RECIPES FROM THE PARADISE ISLANDS

Edited by Beverley Le Blanc

CHARTWELL
BOOKS, INC.

A QUINTET BOOK

Published by Chartwell Books
A Division of Book Sales, Inc.
114, Northfield Avenue
Edison, New Jersey 08837

This edition produced for sale in the U.S.A., its
territories and dependencies only.

ISBN 0-7858-0566-7

This book was designed and produced by
Quintet Publishing Limited
6 Blundell Street
London N7 9BH

Creative Director: Richard Dewing
Designer: Peter Laws
Project Editor: Diana Steedman

Typeset in Great Britain by
Central Southern Typesetters, Eastbourne
Manufactured in China
by Regent Publishing Services Ltd
Printed in China
by Leefung-Asco Printers Ltd

CONTENTS

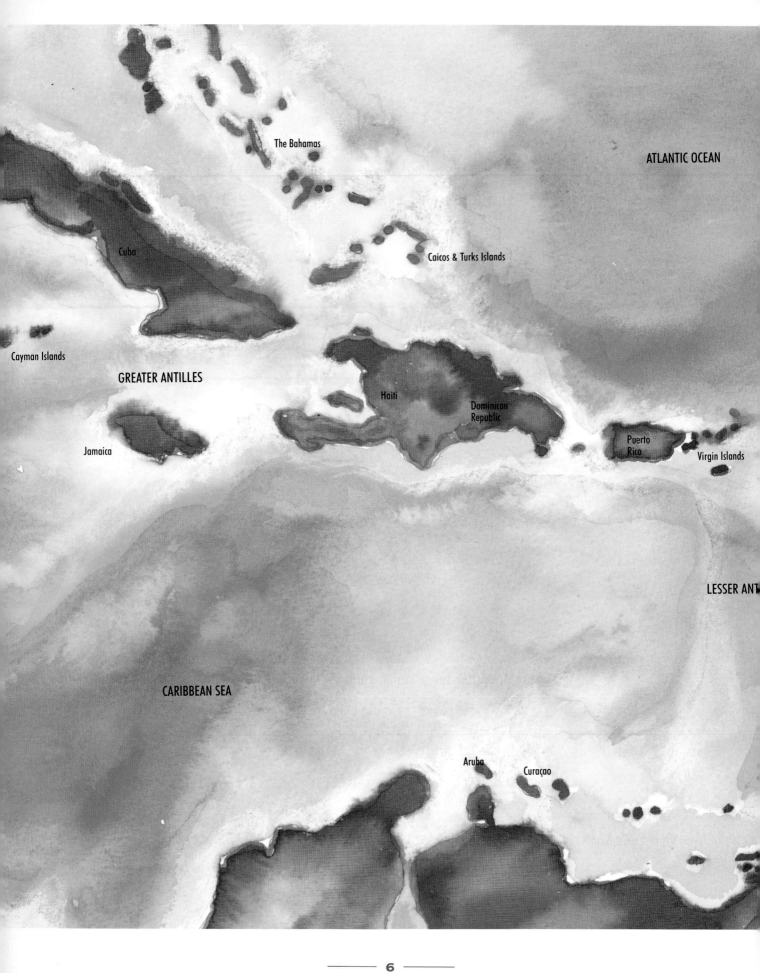

ATLANTIC OCEAN

The Bahamas

Cuba

Caicos & Turks Islands

Cayman Islands

GREATER ANTILLES

Haiti

Dominican Republic

Puerto Rico

Virgin Islands

Jamaica

LESSER ANT

CARIBBEAN SEA

Aruba

Curaçao

Introduction

The map on the left shows several Caribbean islands, labeled from top to bottom: artin, Antigua, Montserrat, evis, uadeloupe, Dominica, Martinique, St Lucia, St Vincent, Barbados, Grenada, Tobago, Trinidad.

When Christopher Columbus reached the Caribbean islands in 1492, he thought he had found the Garden of Eden. He was overwhelmed by the beauty of the islands: the richness of the vegetation, the variety of fruits, the exotic scented flowers, and the singing of the birds.

The chain of Caribbean islands, stretching 2,500 miles from the southern edge of Florida to the northern coast of Venezuela, consists of more than 7,000 islands. Some are little more than rocks in the sea, while others are very big—Cuba being the largest. The next largest island is Hispaniola, which comprises Haiti and the Dominican Republic, followed by Jamaica and Puerto Rico. These four islands and some 25 other large ones, such as Trinidad, Guadeloupe, Martinique, Barbados, and St. Lucia, are known as the Caribbean islands, the West Indies, or the Antilles (a name given by fourteenth-century Europeans to a group of imaginary islands in the Atlantic).

One of the most exciting aspects of Caribbean culture is its cuisine. In the Caribbean, "creole" is defined as "mixed and born on the islands." Caribbean cooking can therefore be termed "creole cuisine", because it is a mix of cooking from all the islands. Caribbean dishes are spicy mixtures of meats, fish, and vegetables. The exotic fruits of the islands are coconuts, guavas, mangoes, papayas, pineapples, bananas, custard apples, star fruit, soursops, mamey sapatos,

tamarind, ugli, passion fruits, and avocados. Vegetables found on the islands are christophenes, eggplants, pumpkins, okras, plantains, breadfruits, and ackees. The peoples of the Caribbean eat a lot of root vegetables such as yams, cassavas, sweet potatoes, and dasheens. The fruits of the tropical sea are the local spiny lobster, conch, shrimp, crabs, kingfish, and other exotic seafood.

Caribbean culture and cuisine have been shaped by four waves of settlers that affected all the islands. The Caribbean islands have been influenced by the Amerindians (Arawaks and Caribs), Europeans (Spanish, British, French, and Dutch), Africans, and Orientals (Indians and Chinese).

About 2,000 years ago, the native inhabitants of the region, the Arawak and the Carib tribes, who originated from Venezuela and Guyana, settled in the Caribbean islands. They were dispersed by European settlers in the form of Spanish soldiers, English pirates, Dutch merchants, Irishmen, Scotsmen, and Frenchmen who left Europe following the voyages of Christopher Columbus. The Europeans later brought African slaves across from the Congo, Guinea, and the Gold Coast to work in their Caribbean sugarcane plantations. The Africans were followed by Orientals, who came as indentured servants from China and India.

The first influence on the Caribbean islands was, therefore, a primitive one. The Amerindians were farmers who grew crops like corn, cassava (which they used to make bread), sweet potatoes, arrowroot, beans, and bell and chili peppers. Others gathered wild fruits such as guavas, pineapples, and cashew fruits, and fished or hunted. A favorite dish was pepperpot—a mixed meat and vegetable stew. Now pepperpot is made only with mixed meats, hot pepper, and cassareep (the boiled juice of grated cassava).

The Amerindians' food was not sufficient for the Europeans, so Columbus asked for flour, meat, oil, vinegar, and wine to be sent from Spain. The Spanish colonists brought with them many fruits, vegetables, and crops that, funnily enough, we now associate with the

Caribbean, such as breadfruit, limes, oranges, mangoes, bananas, coconut, tamarind, sugarcane, ginger, coffee, and rice. Several Spanish dishes still feature in Caribbean cuisine, such as escovitch (page 30), or pickled fish, and *baccalaitos* or stamp and go (page 23), which are salt cod fish cakes. Barbados has retained much of the British influence. Jug jug (page 132)—traditionally served at Christmas—was brought to the island by Scottish people exiled after plotting rebellion in 1685. It is a version of the Scots dish known as haggis, and is made from salted meats, pigeon peas, herbs, and ground millet. The islands of Guadeloupe and Martinique are still part of France, and have a strong French flavor to their cooking. The Dutch have given the Caribbean one of its most interesting dishes—*keshy yana*, commonly known today as shrimp-stuffed Edam cheese (page 69).

The third wave—the African slaves—also greatly influenced Caribbean cuisine. The slaves brought with them pigeon peas, yams, okras, and taros. More importantly, they developed a style of cooking that is the basis of Caribbean cooking today.

As they were given only very small portions of salted meat and fish, they started to supplement their diet by growing their own food. The food given to them had little or no taste, so they found ingenious ways in which to flavor it with seasonings and pungent spices. Today, the main ingredient in the English-speaking islands for a stew is "a bunch of sive," which is made up of scallions tied in a bunch with parsley, coriander leaves, and thyme. The Spanish-speaking islands use *sofrito*—a sauce made from annatto seeds, coriander leaves, green bell peppers, onions, garlic, and tomatoes. Ginger, nutmeg, cloves, allspice, cinnamon, and hot chili peppers are widely used on all the islands. Many of the traditional dishes have survived, such as callaloo (page 40), crab and greens soup.

The fourth influence on Caribbean food came in the early 1800s. There was pressure from England on the European colonists to free their slaves and, in 1848 and 1838 respectively, the French and English

colonies granted emancipation to all the slaves. Although the ex-slaves were then offered wages for their work, many refused to work in the fields, especially in Trinidad. Plantation owners, desperately needing a labor force, transported large numbers of indentured servants from India and China. As a result, curry gradually became as much a Caribbean dish as it is an Indian one. Roti (page 27), or *dhalpour*, is another favorite in Trinidad and Jamaica. Chinese spare ribs, vegetables, and noodles are popular dishes in Trinidad. Maybe this also explains why, despite the variety of vegetables grown in the Caribbean, such as breadfruit, eddoes, cassavas, sweet potatoes, and plantains, which are eaten ripe *and* green, rice is also a very important food for many West Indians. It is served at almost every meal with meat, fish, and vegetables.

When we talk of Caribbean cooking, the food of Guyana and Surinam must be included. Their cuisines are similar to that of the Caribbean islands. Although geographically these two countries are in South America, culturally they form part of the Caribbean.

Tropical Ingredients

Nowadays there are more and more exotic fruits and vegetables in the grocery stores. Plantains, cassavas, coconuts, mangoes, avocados, star fruit, guavas, papayas, and pineapples can be obtained in any specialty West Indian store, and many are now found in supermarkets, too. Even so, it is not always obvious how to recognize, choose, and prepare all the tropical ingredients, so here are some tips.

ACKEE

Ackee is the fruit of an evergreen tree introduced into Jamaica from West Africa. It is reddish-yellow in color, and when ripe it bursts open to display shiny black seeds covered by a creamy-yellow flesh—this is the only edible section, and it has a soft texture resembling scrambled eggs. The fruit must *only* be eaten perfectly ripe—unripe *and* overripe ackee can be poisonous.

ALLSPICE

This flavoring is also known as pimento seed. It is the dark reddish-brown berry of a tree indigenous to Jamaica. After the berries are dried in the sun, they look like large peppercorns, but the scent and flavor are similar to a blend of cinnamon, cloves, and nutmeg, hence the name.

ANNATTO

A rusty red dried seed from the tropical annatto tree. It is used to color and flavor cooking oil. To make annatto liquid dissolve the dried seeds in water.

ARROWROOT

A white starchy powder obtained from the underground stalk of a plant grown mainly in the Caribbean island of St. Vincent. It is used for thickening soups, sauces, and stews.

AVOCADO

It is commonly known as "pear" throughout the Caribbean as it is a pear-shaped fruit with creamy flesh and a thick green skin. Avocados can be bought when still firm. If you want to test the ripeness of an avocado, put it in the palm of your hand and squeeze it gently; when it yields to gentle pressure, it is ready to eat. To prepare an avocado, cut it in half lengthwise. Gently twist the halves apart to loosen the pit. Remove the pit with a knife. Rub the exposed flesh with lemon or lime juice to prevent it discoloring.

BEANS

Islanders use the term peas for both peas and beans. Rice 'n' Peas is a dish made with rice and kidney beans or pigeon peas.

BONIATO

A white-fleshed tuber, this is a particular type of tropical sweet potato. It has a smooth texture when cooked and is only slightly sweet. Try to buy small boniato because they're more tender than larger ones. If you cannot find these, use sweet or white regular potatoes.

BREADFRUIT

A large round or oval green fruit used as a vegetable. It is best used when the skin is green rather than brown. The central core should be removed and the cream-colored flesh eaten as a starchy vegetable, boiled, roasted, or fried.

CALABAZA

This large squash the size of a soccer ball with orange flesh is usually sold in wedges that look like pieces of pumpkin, although the texture and flavor of calabaza is sweeter. You can usually find this squash in West Indian grocers and marketstalls. Hubbard or butternut squashes make good substitutes.

CALLALOO

The name given to the leaves of the dasheen or taro plant with which the soup of the same name (page 40) is made. If you can't find any, spinach is a good substitute.

CASHEW

An evergreen tree and shrub native to the West Indies. It bears a reddish, pear-shaped cashew apple, from the bottom of which grows the kidney-shaped nut; this is edible only when roasted.

CASSAREEP

This is an essential part of the popular dish Pepperpot (page 43). It is the juice obtained from grated cassava and flavored with cinnamon, cloves, and brown sugar.

To make 6 tablespoons, you need 2 pounds of young cassava root. Peel off the brown bark with a small sharp knife to reveal the white flesh of the cassava root. Cut the cassava root in half, and finely grate half of it into a deep bowl lined with a double thickness of dampened cheesecloth. Bring the ends of the cloth together to enclose the pulp, and twist very tightly to squeeze the cassava juice into the bowl; discard the pulp. Grate and squeeze the rest of the cassava in the same way.

Pour the liquid into a small skillet and cook it over medium heat for about 1 minute, stirring constantly, until the cassareep is smooth and thick. Cassareep should be made fresh each time you need it.

CASSAVA

Also known as yuca, manioc, tapioca, and mandioca. This is a long, irregularly shaped root with a dark brown, rough, bark-like skin and hard white starchy flesh. It is an important item in the diet of many West Indians, and can be eaten boiled, baked, or fried.

CHRISTOPHENE

Also known as cho-cho, choyote, chayote, and tropical squash. This is a pear-shaped fruit with a single large seed in the center. The skin varies in color from white to pale yellow or bright green. The flesh is cooked as a vegetable, and has a taste similar to zucchini.

COCONUT

When you buy a coconut, shake it to make sure it has liquid inside—this is a sign that the coconut is fresh.

To open the coconut, puncture two of its "eyes"—the darker dots on one end—with a small, sharp knife or an

SEASONING AND MARINATING

Seasoning and marinating are essential in Caribbean cooking. Few ingredients are cooked without being seasoned a few hours before and left to marinate. Cheap cuts are transformed if they are left to marinate in spices overnight.

◆ Except for steak, all meats—beef, pork, veal, lamb, venison, chicken, hare, or rabbit—should be allowed to marinate for at least 4 hours before cooking.

◆ A good marinade for meat is made from 1¼ cups cold water, 2 crushed garlic cloves, generous pinches of salt and freshly ground black pepper, 1 tablespoon vinegar, and 1 teaspoon chopped thyme.

◆ Fish must be cleaned well in cold water. If it is to be cooked the same day, rinse it well with lime or lemon juice under cold running water. If not, wash it with cold water and vinegar. Remove the scales and any remaining traces of blood, then cut it into steaks or fillets, or leave whole as required.

◆ For the best results, marinate fish for at least 4 hours or overnight. A good marinade for fish is 1 finely chopped scallion, 1 teaspoon chopped chili pepper, generous pinches of salt and freshly ground black pepper, 1 teaspoon chopped thyme, 1 tablespoon vinegar, 2 whole cloves, 3 crushed garlic cloves, and cold water.

ice pick. Drain all the liquid from the coconut, then tap the whole surface of the shell lightly with a hammer. Now give the shell a sharp blow with the hammer. This will open the coconut, and the meat will easily come away from the shell.

HOW TO MAKE COCONUT MILK

Grate the coconut meat. Measure the coconut and stir in an equal amount of hot, but not boiling, water. Cover a bowl with a piece of cheesecloth and strain the coconut through the cloth, pressing down hard on the coconut with a wooden spoon to extract as much liquid as possible. If you measure 1¼ cups of coconut meat to 1¼ cups of water, you should produce 1¼ cups of coconut milk.

CONCH

Known as lambi in the Caribbean. It is an edible sea snail with big horns.

CORIANDER

Known as Chinese parsley or cilantro. It is an aromatic herb, and has a pungent flavor.

CUMIN

It is the yellowish-brown seed of a plant from the parsley family. It is aromatic, and is available whole or ground.

DASHEEN

Also known as taro and cocoyam. It is a tropical plant cultivated for both its underground tubers, which are eaten boiled, roasted or baked, and for its large leaves—known as callaloo leaves—which are used in callaloo (page 40). If dasheen leaves are not available, fresh spinach is a good substitute.

EDDOES

A root vegetable related to dasheen. The underground tubers are similar, though the leaves cannot be eaten.

EGGPLANT

Some eggplants are large, oval-shaped, and purple; others are small and round, or small and long with striped purple skin. It is a vegetable which can be cooked on its own, or with meat and fish.

FLYING FISH

An unusual silver-blue winged fish with a white, slightly salty flesh and a large number of bones. It is found off the coasts of Barbados.

GHEE

Clarified butter—butter with the milk solids removed—that tolerates high temperatures without burning.

GROUPER

More than 50 varieties of this predatory fish are found in Caribbean coastal waters. The moist, firm flesh tastes similar to sea bass, which is a good substitute. Other acceptable substitutes include halibut, whitefish, and snapper.

GUAVA

Here's another so-called "exotic" fruit that is grown in many parts of the world, including Australia, South

THE CARIBBEAN WATERS ARE RICH IN FISH AND SEAFOOD.

Africa and some parts of Southeast Asia, as well as in the Caribbean. This walnut- to apple-sized fruit with lots of edible seeds embedded in the pulp tastes like strawberries to some, bananas to others, pineapple to still others, and like nothing else in the world to others. It's ripe and sweet when it feels like a ripe pear.

Hot Peppers

Hot chili peppers vary in hotness, but you must always be very careful when handling them: they can burn your skin and irritate your eyes, so wear rubber gloves when preparing them.

To prepare hot peppers, rinse them in cold water, then pull out the stalks, cut them in half, and remove the seeds. If the ribs inside the pods are thin, leave them as they are, but if they are firm, remove them with a sharp knife.

To take some of the heat out of chili peppers, soak them in cold, salted water for an hour before using them.

St George's market in Grenada.

Mamay sapote

The sapote family is huge, but Cubans will immediately tell you that there is only one worth considering! The national fruit of the island has a rough, brownish skin, grainy, salmon-colored fruit inside, and a glistening black pit. The taste hints of peaches, cinnamon, and pumpkin.

Mango

The mango is a tropical fruit much used in Caribbean cooking but also delicious eaten raw. The ripe fruit varies in color from green to red. Mangoes are not easy to eat unless you know how to remove the seed. Place the mango flat side down on a board. Cut a thick slice from the top of the fruit as near to the seed as possible. Turn the fruit over. Repeat with the other side. The two halves can then be eaten by scooping out the flesh. The juicy flesh still attached to the seed can be cut off in chunks.

To slice a mango, cut in as far as the seed and down its length, then make another cut into the same central point at an angle to release a slice. Continue cutting slices off one side of the seed, then turn the fruit over to cut slices off the second side. To remove chunks, simply make regular lengthways cuts, then cut across them to mark the size of the chunks. Cut in from one side between the chunks and the seed to separate the pieces of flesh from the seed.

MAWBY BARK
The bark of a tropical tree which has a bitter taste. It is used to make a refreshing drink in the Caribbean.

METHI LEAVES
Also known as fenugreek leaves, methi leaves are taken from a leguminous plant with aromatic seeds.

OKRAS
Known as gumbo, ochro, bamie, or lady's fingers, this plant produces pod-like fruits about 4 inches long. Each pod is oblong in shape and pointed at one end, with a soft and sticky interior. The pod is cooked as a vegetable.

PALM HEART
Tender, ivory-colored shoots obtained from the core at the crown or top of the palm tree. Palm hearts are used as a vegetable or a salad ingredient.

PAPAYA

Also known as pawpaw, this is a large melon-like fruit that ranges in length from 3 to 20 inches. The fruit has a green skin when raw, and a yellow skin, sweet yellow flesh, and black seeds when ripe.

The soft skin contains papain, which is a meat tenderizer. A deliciously simple first course is to serve papaya with ginger.

PASSION FRUIT
An egg-shaped fruit about 2 inches long. When ripe, the leathery skin becomes wrinkled and purple in color. To eat, passion fruit must be cut in half and the juicy yellow seeds scooped out with a spoon.

PIGEON PEAS
Known as goongoo or gunga peas. They are the size of a small garden pea. Young pigeon peas are green, and are available in cans.

PINEAPPLE
One of the most familiar tropical fruits. The best way to peel a pineapple is to remove the spiky leaves from the top, then make slanting cuts downward to remove the skin. It can then be sliced or cut into wedges, removing the core, though, if the pineapple is very ripe, the core should not be removed as it has a very good flavor and texture.

PLANTAIN
A fruit of the banana family, similar in shape but larger and not so sweet; it must be cooked before being eaten. It can be green or yellow in color according to ripeness. Plantains are difficult to handle as the thick skin clings to the fruit. To remove the peel, cut off the ends of the plantain and then halve the trimmed plantain with a sharp knife. Make four evenly spaced lengthwise slits in the skin of each half, cutting through to the flesh from one end to the other. Then, starting at the corner of one slit, lift the skin away, one strip at a time.

POMPANO
A king of the Atlantic coastal waters, pompano's delicate white flesh commands high prices. Sole is a more economical substitute. Pompano fillets are thin, but flavorful with a rich, mild sea flavor. Fillets (no more than ¾-inch thick) of red snapper, sea bass, flounder, or red salmon make good substitutes.

SALTED COD IS A CARIBBEAN SPECIALTY.

RED SNAPPER

Abundantly available in the waters off Cuba. Similar to the grouper and sea bass, red snapper has a lean but firm flesh with a distinctive flavor. If not available, substitute any white, firm-fleshed fish, such as perch, turbot, or sole.

SALT BEEF

Beef preserved in salt. It can be eaten in bread or in recipes.

SALT COD

Originally brought to the Caribbean as food for slaves by the colonists. Of all the salted fish, cod seems to have the best flavor. To remove the salt, wash well and soak for several hours or overnight in cold water.

SEA EGG

The Island name for a white sea urchin.

SORREL

A tropical flower grown throughout the islands. Its fleshy sepal has a faintly acid taste and is used in making drinks, jams, and jellies.

SOURSOP

A large, dark green, heart-shaped fruit with a spiny skin. Its pithy flesh has black seeds and is slightly acidic. It is often used to make drinks or ice creams.

SWEET POTATO

A tuberous vegetable whose skin color ranges from yellow to reddish brown and pink. The flesh may be white, yellow or orange, and can be eaten boiled, baked, fried, or roasted. Ideal for both sweet and savory dishes.

TAMARIND

The fruit of this tree with fern-like branches comes in long, seed-studded pods that look like gigantic brown peapods. The tangy brown pulp inside is edible and is used in Indian, Oriental, and Latin American cooking, as well as Caribbean. Frozen or dried pulp is available in grocery shops catering to those ethnic groups. Tamarind may be eaten as a fruit, rolled in granulated sugar to make a sweetmeat or mixed with water and sugar to make a drink Spanish-speaking people call a *refresco*.

HOW TO MAKE TAMARIND JUICE

Simply simmer ½ cup of crumbled dried tamarind with 1½ cups of water in a heavy small-bottomed saucepan for 10 minutes. Remove the pan from the heat and leave to stand for 1 hour, then strain through a fine strainer into a small bowl. It should be the consistency of heavy cream; if too thick, thin it with a little more water.

TANNIA

A root vegetable of the same family as the dasheen. It is the size of a large baking potato, with dark brown bark-like skin. The firm flesh is white and has a nutty flavor.

TARO

Another name for dasheen.

YAM

These are tubers that grow under large vines known as tropical creepers. Although very like the sweet potato, the yam is not as sweet; the flesh is moister in texture, and the skin is red or brown.

JERK MAGIC

Long before Columbus arrived in the Caribbean islands, the Arawak Indians were preserving meat by rubbing spices and acidic chili peppers into strips of it and then cooking it slowly over an aromatic wood fire until it was bone dry but still flavorful. Later, African slaves in Jamaica adopted the technique when they escaped from their captors and hid in the mountains. It was a variation, after all, of an African technique of cutting game meat into chunks, preparing it to ward off flies, and laying it in the sun to dry. The strips of meat the Maroons, as the ex-slaves were called, smoked in the mountains held up well in the soggy humidity of the tropics and the tradition took firm hold. Early North American trappers, traders, and explorers would likewise learn the preservation technique from the North American Indians. Later, when pioneers pushed westward into lands populated by Mexicans and Western Indians, they coined the word "jerky" for the dried strips of meat that kept them alive during their long journeys. The words "jerk" and "jerky" come from the English corruption of *charqui*, a Spanish word which the conquistadors, in turn, acquired from the Quechua Indians of Peru and Ecuador. (Linguists point out that *escharqui* is what the Indians called it, but the Spanish dropped the first syllable.)

From the survivalist beginnings of jerky a tradition of delicious chargrilled steaks and smoked hams developed, while in Jamaica, Barbados, Trinidad, Tobago, and other islands of the West Indies, an entire culinary art form grew up around jerk. With the advent of refrigeration and modern food processing the need to preserve meat by drying disappeared, but the taste of spiciness and the tenderizing benefits of marinades, pastes, and rubs did not. Today we can cook jerk dishes in a variety of ways, but the early method of slowly grilling or broiling and smoking meats over an aromatic pimento- (allspice-) or guava-wood fire is still practiced. This style of cooking is widespread throughout the Caribbean—in Jamaica, for example, jerk barbecue shacks or pits dot the entire island. The fellow who prepares the meat, poultry, fish, or seafood is called the "jerk mon."

There are many jerk seasoning combinations in the islands today. Most call for a combination of island spices, such as allspice, cinnamon, and nutmeg, plus chili peppers—dry, liquid, or chopped whole—and onion and garlic in some form. Some jerks incorporate acidic liquids such as lime juice or vinegar to add tartness; some include ingredients such as sugar or molasses to add sweetness. And some are very complex, combining all the aforementioned plus herbs, condiments such as Worcestershire sauce, soy sauce, and mustard, and other enhancers from chicken stock to rum.

THE CARIBBEAN ISLANDS REMAIN SOME OF THE WORLD'S MOST IDYLLIC SPOTS.

SIX EASY DRY JERK BLENDS

Once you've tasted some of the recipes in this book, you may want to try some other combinations. The first four recipes here are very simple and use exclusively dry seasonings. The last two incorporate some fresh ingredients, but only the final recipe—Rum Jerk—calls for ingredients to be added at the last minute when you're ready to jerk your dish. Each dry recipe makes a small amount—about 2 tablespoons. When you find one you especially like, make a batch and store it in a tightly sealed jar in the refrigerator.

These jerk blends can be rubbed into just about any meat, fish, or seafood, or used in salads and soups. The dry ones also make nifty seasoning blends to sprinkle on boniato chips and fried green plantains (page 120). Brush croutons with olive oil and then shake them in a paper bag with dry jerk seasoning to coat.

THREE KINDS OF FIRE

2 tsp chili powder
1½ tsp ground cumin
½ tsp cayenne pepper
2 tsp salt

FOUR PEPPERS PLUS

1 tbsp sweet paprika
1 tsp onion powder
1 tsp garlic powder
1 tsp cayenne pepper
½ tsp ground black pepper
½ tsp ground white pepper
½ tsp ground cumin
dash of salt

EASY BAJAN

1 onion, chopped
1 clove garlic, minced
3 scallions, chopped, including some green tops
about ½ in square of chili pepper, chopped
1 tsp minced fresh coriander
1 tsp minced thyme
sprig of marjoram
¼ tsp allspice
½ tsp salt
freshly ground black pepper
dash of Worcestershire sauce

MELANGE

1¼ tbsp sweet paprika
1 tbsp garlic powder
1 tbsp ground black pepper
½ tbsp chili powder
½ tbsp dried thyme
½ tbsp dried oregano
½ tbsp onion powder

EAST-WEST INDIES

3 tsp curry powder
3 tsp sweet paprika
1½ tsp ground cumin
¾ tsp ground allspice
½ tsp chili powder

RUM JERK

2 tbsp garlic powder
2 tsp ground ginger
2 tsp ground allspice
½ tsp ground cinnamon
½ tsp grated nutmeg
2 tsp salt
3 bay leaves, crumbled
2 tsp cayenne pepper
½ cup lime juice
1 onion, sliced
1 cup dark rum
⅔ cup dark brown sugar

Snacks and First Courses

Cheese-Corn Sticks

Stamp and Go

Shrimp and Potato Cakes

Conch Fritters

Beef Patties

Oyster "Cocktails"

Roti

Palm Heart Salad

Chicken and Rice Croquettes

Avocado-Shrimp Boats

Escovitch

Dilled Shrimp in Smoked Kingfish Blanket

Shrimp and Papaya Crepes

Seafood Salad with Black Bean-Papaya Salsa

Lemon and Lime Seafood Salad

Mango-Star Fruit Salad with Ginger Vinaigrette

Salt Cod Salad

Crab-Stuffed Tomatoes

CHEESE-CORN STICKS

MAKES 24

2½ cups water
1 tsp salt
¼ cup yellow cornmeal

¼ cup grated Edam or cheddar
cheese
vegetable oil for frying

Bring the water, with the salt added, to a boil in a saucepan. Gradually add the cornmeal, stirring constantly. Continue to stir for 10 minutes until the mixture is thick.

Remove the pan from the heat. Add the grated cheese and mix it in well, then leave the mixture to cool completely.

Wetting your hands in cold water from time to time, make the mixture into sticks about 3 inches long and 1 inch wide. Lay on waxed paper and chill for 3 to 24 hours.

When ready to fry, preheat the oven to its lowest temperature and line a baking dish with aluminum foil.

Heat a little vegetable oil in a skillet and fry 4 sticks at a time, turning them over and cooking them until they are crisp. Transfer the cooked sticks to the baking dish, and keep them warm in the oven while you fry the rest. Serve them hot.

STAMP AND GO

MAKES 24

Once sold from humble seaside shacks in Jamaica, these codfish cakes were wrapped in paper and stamped "paid"—hence the name Stamp and Go. People on the Spanish-speaking islands call salted cod bacalao and eat very similar cod fritters. Cod was salted out of necessity in the days before refrigeration and the custom continues today.

½ lb salt cod

2 tbsp vegetable oil mixed with
* 1 tsp liquid annatto (page 12)*

1 onion, finely chopped

1 cup all-purpose flour

1 tsp baking powder

½ tsp salt

1 egg, lightly beaten

½ cup milk

2½ tsp melted butter or
* margarine*

½ fresh chili pepper, finely
* chopped*

vegetable oil for frying

Soak the salt cod in a glass bowl for 12 hours, changing the water 3 or 4 times during this time.

Drain the cod and rinse it under cold running water, then put it into a large saucepan and cover with fresh cold water. Bring to a boil, then reduce the heat and simmer for 20 minutes.

Drain off the water and lift out the fish. Remove the skin and bones and flake the flesh into a bowl.

Heat the annatto-flavored oil in a large saucepan. Add the onion and fry until it is soft. Remove the pan from the heat and set it to one side.

Sift the flour, baking powder, and salt into a large mixing bowl. Add the egg, milk, and melted butter or margarine and mix. Add the cooked onion and oil, the flaked cod, and the chili pepper. Mix to form a batter.

Pour vegetable oil to a depth of 1/2 inch into a large skillet and heat until very hot. Drop the batter, a tablespoon at a time, into the hot oil and fry for 3 minutes, turning the fish cakes over so they cook evenly. Drain on paper towels. These fish cakes can be eaten hot or cold.

SHRIMP AND POTATO CAKES

MAKES 14

*2 baking potatoes, peeled and
  quartered*
2½ tbsp butter or margarine
1½ cups grated cheddar cheese
1 egg yolk
*3 tbsp finely chopped fresh
  parsley*
1 tsp salt
freshly ground black pepper

1 onion, finely chopped
*1 lb cooked shelled shrimp,
  deveined and chopped*
½ cup all-purpose flour
1 egg, lightly beaten
*⅓ cup soft, fresh white bread
  crumbs*
vegetable oil for frying

Boil the potatoes in salted water until they are soft. Drain and mash them with a fork. Add two-thirds of the butter or margarine, the cheese, egg yolk, parsley, salt, and freshly ground black pepper to taste. Mix well until the mixture is well blended and smooth.

Melt the remaining butter or margarine in a skillet. Add the onion and cook for 5 minutes, then add the shrimp and cook for 1 minute longer.

Add the contents of the skillet to the potato mixture and mix together well. Leave the mixture to cool, then cover and chill it for at least 1 hour.

Form the mixture into round patterns, approximately 1½ inch in diameter, with your hands. Roll each pasty in flour and brush with the beaten egg. Dip each in the bread crumbs and put the finished cakes on waxed paper.

Deep-fry 5 cakes at a time, turning them over when they are golden. Drain them on paper towels to absorb excess oil. Serve hot or cold.

CONCH FRITTERS

SERVES 4

1 lb conch, abalone, or squid,
  blanched and finely ground in
  a food processor
2 green bell peppers, cored,
  seeded and finely sliced
2 small onions, finely diced
2 tsp baking powder
3 celery sticks, finely chopped
1 large egg
2 tsp chopped fresh coriander

½ tsp cayenne pepper
2 tsp Worcestershire sauce
1 clove garlic, crushed
pinch of dried thyme
½ tsp freshly ground black
  pepper
pinch of baking soda
milk
1½ cups self-rising flour
vegetable oil for deep-frying

Mix together the conch or substitute, peppers, onions, baking powder, celery, egg, coriander, cayenne, Worcestershire, garlic, thyme, black pepper, baking soda, and milk. Slowly stir in flour to make a batter, then cover and refrigerate overnight.

Heat 2–3 inches vegetable oil deep to 350°F in a deep, heavy-bottomed saucepan or deep-fat fryer. Drop soupspoonfuls of batter into oil without crowding the pan. If fritters bob to top of oil, submerge with tongs or a slotted spoon. Remove them from oil when they are golden brown on all sides. Drain on paper towels and serve immediately.

BEEF PATTIES

MAKES 12

FOR THE PASTRY

4 cups all-purpose flour
2 tsp turmeric
1 tsp salt
1 cup butter, softened, or
  margarine
3 tbsp cold water

FOR THE FILLING

2 tbsp vegetable oil
1 onion, finely chopped
2 scallions, finely chopped
2 garlic cloves, crushed
2 fresh chili peppers, seeded and
  finely chopped

¾ lb ground beef
4 tomatoes, skinned and
  chopped
¼ tsp turmeric
¼ tsp ground cumin
¼ tsp ground ginger
¼ tsp ground cinnamon
¼ tsp ground cloves
¼ tsp ground cardamom
½ cup water
salt and freshly ground black
  pepper

FOR THE GLAZE

2 egg yolks, beaten

First make the pastry dough. Sift the flour, turmeric, and salt into a bowl. Add the butter or margarine, and mix well until the mixture resembles bread crumbs. Mix in just enough of the cold water to form a stiff dough. Wrap the dough in plastic wrap and chill for 2 hours.

For the filling, heat the oil in a saucepan and fry the onion until it is soft. Add the scallions, garlic, and chili peppers and cook for 2 minutes longer.

Add the beef, tomatoes, and spices, and season to taste with salt and freshly ground black pepper. Reduce the heat, stir in ½ cup water, and simmer for 20 minutes.

Remove from the heat and leave the mixture to cool.

Meanwhile, preheat the oven to 400°F. Roll out the dough and cut out 12 circles approximately 7 inches in diameter using a saucer.

Put 2 tablespoons of the filling on one side of each dough circle, then fold the other half over so the edges meet. Crimp the edges together with a fork to seal. Place on a baking tray lined with aluminum foil, and brush the tops with the beaten egg yolk glaze. Bake in the center of the oven for 30 minutes until golden brown. Serve at once.

OYSTER COCKTAILS

SERVES 6

24 fresh oysters

4 tsp lime juice

½ tsp hot pepper sauce

1 onion, finely chopped

2 tsp salt

1 small tomato, skinned and
    finely chopped

1 tsp olive oil

Rinse the oysters under cold running water, then leave them to soak in a bowl of cold water with 1 teaspoon of the lime juice for 5 minutes. Drain off the water.

Mix the remaining lime juice with the hot pepper sauce, onion, salt, tomato, and olive oil in a bowl. Add the oysters and leave to marinate for 5 minutes.

Chill for 10 minutes before serving.

ROTI

SERVES 10

4 cups split peas

1 tbsp salt

½ tsp ground turmeric

1 tbsp cumin seeds

¼ tsp chili powder (optional)

6 cups all-purpose flour

6 tsp baking powder

¼ cup ghee (clarified butter) or
    margarine

vegetable oil for frying

Rinse the split peas and put them in a saucepan full of water with half of the salt and the turmeric. Bring to a boil and cook for 10 minutes, or until the split peas are half-cooked.

Drain off the water and process the split peas in a blender or food processor to form a powder, not a paste.

Add the cumin and chili, then set the mixture on one side.

Sift the flour, the remaining salt, and the baking powder into a large mixing bowl. Mix in the ghee or margarine, working it in until it is well blended. Add just enough warm water, little by little, until you have a soft dough. Knead the dough for 5 minutes.

Form the dough into small balls and set aside on a floured board. Flour your hands well and flatten the balls into thick circles. Put 1 or 2 tablespoons of the split-pea mixture into the center of each circle and close the dough over it, making sure the mixture is sealed inside the dough. Then, roll each with a floured rolling pin on a floured board to make a circle about 5 inches in diameter and ¾ inch thick.

Brush the tops with oil and place them, oiled side down, on a hot griddle. Cook the roti for 3 minutes, then brush their tops with oil and turn over. Cook both sides until they are lightly browned. Remove them to a clean dish towel and wrap to keep them warm.

PALM HEART SALAD

SERVES 6

4-oz can palm hearts, drained

2 green mangoes, peeled and
   thinly sliced

½ cucumber, peeled and thinly
   sliced

2 ripe avocado pears

½ fresh chili pepper, deseeded
   and thinly sliced

FOR THE DRESSING

juice of 1 lime or lemon

1 tsp mustard powder

1 tsp sugar

4 tbsp olive oil

salt and freshly ground black
   pepper

First make the dressing. Mix half the lime or lemon juice
with the mustard powder, sugar, olive oil, salt, and freshly
ground black pepper.

Next, make the salad. Chop the palm hearts into slices.
Put the palm heart slices, mango, and cucumber into a glass
serving bowl. Peel, seed, and thinly slice the avocados, and
add them to the bowl. Stir in the chili, together with the
rest of the lime or lemon juice to prevent the ingredients
discoloring.

Serve the salad with the dressing on the side.

CHICKEN AND RICE CROQUETTES

MAKES 24

4 cups diced cooked chicken

2½ cups cooked rice (about 2 cups uncooked)

½ onion, chopped

2 tsp tomato catsup

salt and freshly ground black pepper

½ tsp paprika

3 eggs, beaten

1 cup dried bread crumbs

vegetable oil for frying

hot pepper sauce for serving

Mix all the ingredients together, except the eggs, bread crumbs, and the oil. Roll the mixture into small balls, then dip each one in the beaten egg and roll in the bread crumbs to coat them.

Heat some oil in a saucepan and deep-fry the croquettes until they are golden brown. Serve at once with hot pepper sauce on the side.

AVOCADO-SHRIMP BOATS

SERVES 4

FOR THE MANGO SALSA

2 mangoes, peeled, pitted, and diced

½ cup chopped red onion

½ cup chopped red bell pepper

2 jalapeño chilis, seeded and chopped

3 tbsp fresh lime juice

FOR THE AVOCADO BOATS

4 oz shelled shrimp

2 ripe but firm avocados

To make the salsa, put all the ingredients in a bowl and stir together. Cover and chill for at least 1 hour.

Mix the shrimp with the salsa. Cut the avocados in half and scoop out the pits.

Mound the salsa into the avocado halves. If absolutely necessary, scoop out a little of the avocado flesh to make room for the salsa. Serve at once.

ESCOVITCH

SERVES 6

This popular pickled fish dish is featured on menus on most Islands, a hold over from the days before refrigeration.

4 onions, thinly sliced

2 carrots, scraped and sliced

2 green bell peppers, cored, seeded, and chopped

2 bay leaves

½ tsp fresh chili pepper, crushed

2 tsp salt

freshly ground black pepper

6 tbsp white-wine vinegar

5 tbsp olive oil

1¼ cups cold water

2 lb red snapper, skinned and filleted

Put the onions, carrots, green peppers, bay leaves, chili pepper, salt and freshly ground black pepper to taste, vinegar, 1½ tablespoons of the oil, and the water into a large saucepan. Bring to a boil over high heat, then reduce the heat and simmer until the vegetables are tender.

Meanwhile, heat the remaining oil in a large skillet. Add the fish fillets and cook each side for 2 minutes, or until golden brown. Transfer the fish to a shallow heatproof dish. Pour the contents of the saucepan over the fish and leave to cool.

Serve with baked yams or breadfruit

DILLED SHRIMP IN SMOKED KINGFISH BLANKET

SERVES 4 TO 6

Almost any thinly sliced smoked fish can be substituted for the Caribbean kingfish—just make certain skin and bones have been removed. Choose the plumpest shrimp, however, so that the treasure inside the "blanket" can be fully savored.

2 tbsp fresh lime or lemon juice

½ tsp salt

1 tbsp chopped fresh coriander

5 tbsp olive oil

1 tbsp chopped fresh dill

freshly ground white pepper

24 cooked shrimp, shelled and deveined

4 oz smoked kingfish, thinly sliced and chilled

TO GARNISH

fresh dill sprigs (optional)

cherry tomatoes (optional)

Combine the lime or lemon juice, salt, coriander, olive oil, dill, and pepper in a glass bowl. Add the shrimp, cover, and marinate for 2 hours.

Cut each slice of fish lengthwise into strips ¼ inch wide.

Wind a fish strip around each shrimp and fasten with a toothpick. Garnish and serve.

SHRIMP AND PAPAYA CRÊPES

SERVES 4 TO 5

1 lb shrimp in shells

1 papaya

3 tbsp unsalted butter

1 small leek, trimmed and thinly
    sliced

2-in piece fresh gingerroot,
    grated

2 tbsp dry vermouth

1 tbsp lime juice (optional)

salt and freshly ground white
    pepper

1 cup sour cream

2 to 3 tbsp chopped fresh dill or
    fennel

FOR THE CRÊPE BATTER

1 cup all-purpose flour

1 egg

pinch of salt

1 tbsp corn oil

1¼ cups milk

vegetable oil for frying

First make the crêpes. Beat the flour, egg, salt, and oil together, then gradually beat in the milk; this quantity should make 8 to 10 fairly small, thin crêpes.

Heat a little oil in a small skillet and pour in sufficient batter to cover the bottom thinly. Cook both sides of the crêpes. Keep hot until all the batter has been used.

Peel the shrimp. Peel the papaya, then halve them and remove the pits. Cut the flesh into fairly small dice.

Melt the butter in a skillet. Add the leek and cook until it is slightly soft, then add the ginger and cook for a few seconds. Add the vermouth, shrimp, and papaya to the pan with the lime juice, if used, and salt and pepper. Heat through gently.

Fold each crêpe into quarters and, dividing the filling between the crêpes, use a pocket of each crêpe to hold the filling. Place on a heated dish and put in a warm oven until ready to serve.

Mix the sour cream with the dill or fennel, add salt and pepper to taste, and serve with the crêpes.

LIKE CARIBBEAN COOKING, CARNIVAL TIME IS COLORFUL AND EXUBERANT.

Seafood Salad with Black Bean-Papaya Salsa

SERVES 4

mixed salad greens
12 to 16 oz broiled salmon,
　chilled

For the Black Bean-Papaya Salsa

16-oz can of black beans, rinsed
　and drained
1 papaya, peeled, pitted, and
　diced

2 roasted chili peppers, peeled,
　and chopped
½ cup chopped red pepper
½ cup chopped red onion
¼ cup chopped fresh cilantro
1 tsp finely minced fresh ginger
¼ cup fresh lime juice
1 tsp crushed dried red chili
salt and pepper to taste

To make the salsa, mix all the ingredients together. Let stand for 30 minutes, then taste and adjust the seasoning.

Clean and tear the salad greens and divide them between 4 plates.

Break the salmon into chunks, removing any bones. Divide the salmon among the plates. Top each salad with ½ cup Black Bean-Papaya Salsa. Serve at once.

LEMON AND LIME SEAFOOD SALAD

SERVES 4

1 lb fresh grouper or other firm,
  white fish
2 fresh scallops
8 oz red snapper
6 oz prepared fresh squid
6 oz fresh shelled shrimp
6 tbsp chopped fresh parsley
2 tbsp chopped fresh tarragon

4 tbsp chopped fresh mint
3 tbsp olive oil
juice of 1 lemon
juice of 1 lime
bunch of scallions, trimmed and
  chopped
salt and freshly ground pepper

Clean and skin the grouper and cut it into small pieces. Clean the scallops. Remove the red snapper from the bone and cut the flesh into cubes. Rinse the squid under running water and cut into rings.

Poach all the seafood in lightly salted water for a short time until just tender. Drain well, cool, and place in a mixing bowl with the shelled shrimp.

Place all the herbs in a bowl with the oil, citrus juices, scallions and salt and freshly ground pepper. Stir together and pour over the fish and lightly toss. Leave for at least 30 minutes for the flavors to develop.

MANGO-STAR FRUIT SALAD WITH
GINGER VINAIGRETTE

SERVES 4

This vinaigrette also tastes great sprinkled over boniato chips, fried green plantains, green salads, and even jerk dishes.

4 mangoes, cubed

4 star fruit, sliced crosswise into
   star shapes

1 tbsp grated fresh gingerroot

½ cup olive oil

½ cup cider vinegar

2 tbsp fresh lime juice

1 tsp Dijon-style mustard

1 tsp minced fresh coriander

¼ tsp minced scallion

¼ tsp salt

¼ tsp freshly ground black
   pepper

Combine the mangoes and star fruit and chill.

Purée the ginger, olive oil, vinegar, lime juice, mustard, coriander, scallion and salt and pepper in a blender or food processor until smooth.

When you are ready to serve, drizzle the vinaigrette over the fruit.

SALT COD SALAD

SERVES 6

½ lb salt cod, soaked overnight
   and drained
juice of 1 lime or lemon
1 onion, finely chopped
3 tomatoes, chopped
3 tbsp olive oil
2 hard-boiled eggs, chopped
1 fresh chili pepper, seeded and

finely chopped
2 tbsp finely chopped scallions
1 green bell pepper, cored,
   seeded and finely chopped
2 tbsp finely chopped fresh
   parsley
freshly ground black pepper

Boil the cod for 20 minutes or until it is tender and flakes easily.

Drain off the water and rinse under cold running water. Remove the skin and bones, and flake the flesh into a glass bowl. Add the lime or lemon juice, onion, tomatoes, olive oil, eggs, chili pepper, scallions, green pepper, parsley, and freshly ground black pepper. Mix together well.

When the mixture has cooled, cover the bowl with plastic wrap and refrigerate overnight.

Serve the next day on crackers, fresh bread, or small, toasted slices of bread.

CRAB-STUFFED TOMATOES

SERVES 2

Use a very good prepared hot pepper sauce from the Caribbean. A touch of hot, hot, hot is what gives the dish its special island flair.

1 lb crabmeat, thawed and drained if frozen

2 large ripe tomatoes, seeded and chopped

3/4 cup diced cucumber

2 hard-boiled eggs, chopped

2/3 cup mayonnaise

4 tbsp hot pepper sauce

2 tbsp sour cream

2 tsp lime juice

1 tbsp finely snipped fresh chives

salt and freshly ground black pepper

2 large ripe tomatoes

1 round lettuce, rinsed and dried

Blend together the crab, chopped tomatoes, cucumber, and eggs, then cover and chill. Blend together the mayonnaise, hot pepper sauce, sour cream, lime juice, chives and salt and pepper, then cover and chill.

Without cutting through the bottoms, core the whole tomatoes and cut them into sixths, forming tulip shapes.

Line 2 plates with the lettuce, center the tomatoes on the lettuce, and mound the crab salad on top. Serve the salad with remaining sauce.

Soups

CALLALOO

GREEN PIGEON PEA SOUP

PUMPKIN SOUP

PEPPERPOT

BLACK BEAN SOUP

CHICKEN AND VEGETABLE SOUP

TOMATO AND SWEET POTATO SOUP

PEANUT SOUP

TOMATO AND ORANGE SOUP

AVOCADO SOUP

BREADFRUIT SOUP

GRILLED SEAFOOD SOUP

COCONUT AND SHRIMP SOUP

SPICY CHICKEN SOUP

PINEAPPLE AND MANGO BISQUE

ICED PASSION FRUIT SOUP WITH YOGURT AND VANILLA

CALLALOO

SERVES 6

½ lb dasheen leaves or 1 lb fresh
  dasheen or spinach
2½ tbsp butter or margarine
1 onion, finely chopped
2 garlic cloves, crushed
1 fresh chili pepper, seeded and
  finely chopped
¼ lb okra, trimmed and sliced
1 sprig fresh thyme

3¾ cups chicken stock
1¼ cups coconut milk (page 14)
salt and freshly ground black
  pepper
½ lb crabmeat, fresh, canned or
  frozen
dash of hot pepper sauce

Wash the dasheen or spinach leaves, then drain and shred.

Melt the butter or margarine in a large saucepan over medium heat. Add the onion and garlic and cook for 5 minutes, stirring occasionally until soft and golden. Add the chili pepper, okra, and thyme, and cook for 5 minutes longer, stirring constantly.

Stir in the dasheen or spinach leaves and cook for 3 minutes, turning them in the pan to ensure they are evenly cooked. Pour the stock and coconut milk over the leaves, season with salt and freshly ground black pepper, and bring to a boil. Lower the heat, cover the pan, and simmer for 30 minutes.

Add the crabmeat and cook for 5 minutes longer until the mixture has heated through. Taste and adjust the seasoning if necessary, and stir in the pepper sauce. Serve on its own in warmed soup bowls.

GREEN PIGEON PEA SOUP

SERVES 6

½ cup butter or margarine
1 medium onion, finely chopped
1 fat garlic clove, crushed
1 large, firm tomato, peeled,
  seeded, and chopped
1 small green bell pepper,
  seeded, white pith removed,
  and finely chopped
1 cup diced cooked boned
  chicken

1 lb fresh pumpkin, peeled,
  seeded, and diced
2½ cups chicken stock
16-oz can green pigeon peas
  with liquid
salt and freshly ground black
  pepper

Melt the butter or margarine in a large saucepan. Add the onion and garlic and fry over a medium heat until soft.

Add the tomato, green pepper, and chicken. Cover the pan and simmer for 5 minutes.

Add the pumpkin, chicken stock, and green pigeon peas. Bring to a boil, then reduce the heat and simmer for 20 minutes, or until the soup thickens and the pumpkin is tender. The soup should remain lumpy.

Season to taste with salt and freshly ground black pepper, and serve at once.

CALLALOO IS A TRADITIONAL DISH OF BARBADOS.

PUMPKIN SOUP

SERVES 4 – 6

2 lb pumpkin, peeled, seeded,
   and cut into 1-inch cubes
salt and freshly ground black
   pepper
2 tbsp butter or margarine
1 large onion, finely chopped
3 scallions, trimmed and finely
   chopped

3 tomatoes, skinned and
   chopped
1 cup coconut milk (page 14)
¼ tsp freshly grated nutmeg
pinch of cayenne pepper
⅔ cup sour cream or yogurt

Put the pumpkin in a saucepan and add enough water (about 3¾ cups) to cover and 1 teaspoon salt. Bring to a boil, then lower the heat and simmer for 20 minutes.

Drain the pumpkin and reserve the cooking liquid.

Melt the butter or margarine in a clean saucepan over medium heat. Add the onion and scallions, and fry them, stirring constantly, for 5 minutes until they are soft and golden. Add the pumpkin, tomatoes, coconut milk, 3 cups of the pumpkin cooking liquid, half the nutmeg, a pinch of cayenne pepper, and salt and freshly ground black pepper. Bring to a boil, then lower the heat, cover, and simmer for 30 minutes.

Remove the pan from the heat and leave the mixture to cool slightly. Purée half the soup at a time in a blender or food processor, then return it to the pan. Heat it through for 5 minutes, then pour the soup into warmed soup bowls and swirl a little of the sour cream or yogurt on top. Sprinkle with the remaining nutmeg and serve at once.

PEPPERPOT

This dish is said to come from Amerindian cuisine and is still eaten on many islands, including Tobago, St. Kitts, and Barbados. It seems a pepperpot is always simmering on the stove in the islands—some West Indians joke that great-great-great grandmother started their pot going some decades ago.

3 lb boiling chicken, trimmed of
  fat and cut into 12 pieces
½ lb fresh pig's trotter
2 quarts water
1½ tsp salt
3 lb boned pork or beef, cut into
  2-in cubes
6 tbsp cassareep (page 13)

1 large onion, sliced
1½ tbsp brown sugar
2 whole, fresh chili peppers
4 whole cloves
2-in piece of cinnamon stick
¼ tbsp dried thyme
2½ tsp malt or distilled vinegar

Put the chicken, pig's trotter, and water into a large saucepan (the water should cover them by about 1 inch). Add the salt and bring to a boil over low heat, skimming off any foam as it collects on the surface. Then, reduce the heat, partially cover the pan, and simmer for about 1 hour or until the chicken is cooked.

Skim as much fat as possible from the surface of the soup. Stir in the pork or beef, cassareep, onion, brown sugar, chili peppers, cloves, cinnamon stick, and thyme. Bring to a boil over high heat, then lower the heat and simmer for 30 minutes, stirring occasionally, until the meat is cooked.

Remove the cloves, cinnamon stick, and chili peppers. Stir in the vinegar and taste, adjusting the seasoning if necessary.

Serve the soup with boiled yam, cassava, or potatoes as accompaniments.

BLACK BEAN SOUP

SERVES 6

1 lb dried black beans

2½ tsp salt

3¾ cups chicken stock

1½ tbsp vegetable oil mixed with
   1 tsp liquid annatto (page 12)

1 medium onion, finely chopped

1 fat garlic clove, finely chopped

1½ cups finely chopped lean
   cooked ham

1 large, firm, ripe tomato,
   peeled, seeded, and finely
   chopped; or 8-oz can crushed
   tomatoes, drained

1½ tbsp malt or distilled vinegar

½ tsp ground cumin

freshly ground black pepper

Rinse the beans under cold running water and drain in a colander. Put the beans in a large saucepan with the salt and enough water to cover the beans by 2 inches. Bring to a boil over high heat, then reduce the heat, partially cover the pan, and simmer for 2 hours or until the beans are tender.

Drain the beans, reserving the liquid, then leave them on one side to cool.

Add enough chicken stock to the reserved cooking liquid from the beans to make 5 cups. Put half the cooked beans in a blender or food processor and grind, but not too finely. Grind the remaining beans. Mix the ground beans with the chicken and bean stock.

Heat the oil in a large saucepan. Add the onion and garlic and fry for 5 minutes, stirring frequently. Stir in the ham, tomato, vinegar, cumin, bean, stock mixture, and freshly ground black pepper to taste. Bring to a boil, then lower the heat and simmer for 15 minutes. Taste to check the seasoning, adjusting if necessary.

Serve the soup piping hot in bowls, accompanied by slices of fresh bread.

CHICKEN AND VEGETABLE SOUP

SERVES 6

3 lb chicken, cut into 8 pieces
3 quarts chicken stock
4 large tomatoes, peeled, seeded, and chopped; or 2 x 16-oz can crushed tomatoes, drained
2 corn cobs, cut into 3-in pieces
2 yams, peeled and chopped into 1-in thick slices

1 cup peeled and diced pumpkin
¼ cup fresh or frozen green peas
2 small chili peppers, seeded and thinly sliced
2½ tsp salt
freshly ground black pepper
1½ tbsp finely snipped fresh chives

Put the chicken pieces and stock into a large saucepan. Bring to a boil over high heat, skimming off the foam with a large spoon. Reduce the heat, partially cover, and simmer for 45 minutes.

Skim the fat from the soup. Add the tomatoes, corn, yams, potatoes, pumpkin, peas, chili peppers, salt and freshly ground black pepper. Bring to the boil, then reduce the heat and simmer for about 20 minutes, or until the chicken and vegetables are cooked.

Taste the soup, adjusting the seasoning if necessary. Stir in the chives, then serve immediately.

TOMATO AND SWEET POTATO SOUP

SERVES 6

1 tbsp oil
1 tbsp butter or margarine
2 onions, finely chopped
1½ cups peeled and diced sweet
  potatoes
2½ cups skinned and finely
  chopped tomatoes
2½ cups chicken stock

1 tsp salt
1 tsp chopped fresh thyme
juice and grated peel of 1 orange
juice and grated peel of 1 lemon
  or lime
freshly ground black pepper
slices of lemon, orange, and
  tomato to garnish

Heat the oil and butter or margarine in a large saucepan. Add the onions and fry them, stirring frequently, until they are soft.

Add the sweet potatoes, tomatoes, chicken stock, salt, thyme, orange juice and peel, lemon or lime juice and peel, and freshly ground black pepper to taste. Bring to a boil, then lower the heat, cover the saucepan, and simmer for 25 minutes.

Purée the soup in a blender or food processor, then return it to the saucepan and simmer for 5 minutes longer to heat it through.

Serve it in warmed soup bowls, garnished with a slice of tomato, orange, and lemon.

PEANUT SOUP

1/4 cup butter or margarine

1 onion, grated

1 celery stick, chopped

1 garlic clove, crushed

1 sprig fresh thyme, chopped

1 tbsp all-purpose flour

3¾ cups chicken stock

½ cup crunchy peanut butter or
  2¼ cups coarsely ground
  peanuts

2 cups milk

2 tsp salt

½ tsp freshly ground black
  pepper

¼ green bell pepper, seeded and
  chopped

Melt the butter or margarine in a large saucepan over low heat. Add the onion, celery, garlic, and thyme and fry for 5 minutes, stirring all the time.

Gradually add the flour and stock, still stirring constantly. Increase the heat, then stir in the peanut butter or peanuts and simmer for 10 minutes.

Reduce the heat and add the milk, salt, and pepper. Simmer for 15 minutes longer.

Serve very hot, garnished with the chopped green pepper

SUNSET AT NEGRIL, JAMAICA.

TOMATO AND ORANGE SOUP

S E R V E S   4

The orange in this soup brings out the sweet-acidic flavor of homegrown tomatoes, if you are lucky enough to have some. Serve with jerk croutons for an extra treat for the taste buds.

2¼ lb ripe tomatoes, blanched,
   peeled, and quartered (or
   canned whole tomatoes,
   undrained)
¼ oz fresh basil leaves
3- x ½-in strip orange peel
2 tbsp chopped scallion (white
   part only)
1 tsp sugar

2 tbsp lime or lemon juice
1 cup orange juice
1 tbsp cornstarch
2 tbsp minced fresh coriander,
   chives, or parsley
salt and freshly ground black
   pepper
jerk croutons (page 19)

Put the tomatoes, basil, orange peel, scallion, sugar and lime or lemon juice in a saucepan. Cover and bring to a boil, then lower the heat immediately and simmer, covered, for 15 minutes.

Remove the orange peel. Purée the mixture in a blender or food processor and strain it if desired to discard seeds.

Return the liquid to the pan. Stir together the orange juice and cornstarch in a small bowl until smooth, then stir into the tomato mixture.

Simmer the soup over medium heat, stirring constantly, until it thickens and comes to a boil. Lower the heat, stir in the coriander, chives, or parsley. Add salt and pepper to taste. Garnish with jerk croutons, if desired.

AVOCADO SOUP

SERVES 4

This easy, no-cook soup is wonderful on a summer day, when avocados are plentiful and cheap. Be sure that the avocados are perfectly ripe, but not overripe, since this soup showcases their flavor.

3 ripe avocados, peeled and
  pitted
1¼ cups chicken broth
1 cup light cream

1 tsp salt
¼ tsp cayenne
1 cup broiled tomato salsa
  (page 138) to serve

Put all the ingredients, except the salsa, in a blender or food processor and purée until smooth.

Transfer the soup to a bowl and chill for at least 2 hours. Although the soup needs to be made at least 2 hours in advance, it does not keep well if it is made more than 8 hours in advance.

Stir well to blend in any darkening on the surface. Serve cold, garnished with a crunchy salsa.

BREADFRUIT SOUP

SERVES 6

4 tbsp butter or margarine
1 onion, finely chopped
1 fat garlic clove, crushed
6 oz fresh breadfruit, peeled,
  cored, and chopped
2½ cups chicken stock

1¼ cups light cream
1 tsp salt
¼ tsp freshly ground black
  pepper
2 tsp finely chopped fresh
  parsley

Melt the butter or margarine in a large saucepan. Add the onion and garlic and fry for 5 minutes, stirring until they are soft.

Add the breadfruit and chicken stock and bring to a boil, then reduce the heat and simmer for 20 minutes, or until the breadfruit is tender.

Put half the mixture in a blender or food processor, together with half of the cream, and blend them together. Tip the purée into a bowl. Repeat for the remainder of the mixture, using the remainder of the cream.

Season the creamy soup with the salt and pepper. Chill until ready to serve, then sprinkle with chopped parsley before serving.

GRILLED SEAFOOD SOUP

SERVES 4

This recipe calls for shrimp and scallops, but you can substitute other grilled or broiled seafood or fish. The size is not important (tiny Bay shrimp are not recommended), although smaller pieces may fall through the grill rack. You can also substitute a different salsa—any smooth, tomato-based one is good. Since the spiciness of the soup depends on the salsa, a fairly hot one is recommended.

¼ lb shrimp, shelled and
    deveined
¾ lb scallops
¼ cup olive oil
¼ cup fresh lime juice
3 cloves garlic, minced
1 tbsp vegetable oil
2 to 2½ cups Basic Cooked Salsa
    (see below)
5 cups clam juice or seafood
    stock
1 tbsp fresh basil or 1 tsp dried
1 tsp fresh thyme or ¼ tsp dried
3 thick slices of onion, separated
    into rings
½ bell pepper, cored, seeded and
    cut into chunks

1 or 2 jalapeño chilis, thinly
    sliced
salt and pepper to taste

FOR THE BASIC COOKED SALSA

2 cups seeded and chopped
    tomatoes
2 cloves garlic, minced
½ cup finely chopped onion
4 jalapeño chilis, chopped, with
    some seeds included
1 tbsp cider vinegar
1 tsp fresh oregano or ¼ tsp
    dried
salt to taste

First make the salsa. Put the tomatoes, garlic, and onion into a saucepan and simmer for 10 to 15 minutes, uncovered, to evaporate excess liquid from the tomatoes. Add the chilis, vinegar, and oregano and simmer for 5 minutes longer. Add salt to taste.

Transfer the salsa to a bowl and leave to cool. Cover and chill for at least 2 hours.

To make the soup, put the seafood in a glass bowl. Mix the olive oil, lime juice, and garlic together, then pour over the seafood and stir so all the pieces are coated. Refrigerate the seafood while you prepare the barbecue. It will be easiest to grill the seafood if it is threaded on skewers (wooden skewers should be soaked in water for 30 minutes to prevent burning) or if you use a special tray for grilling small items.

Mound coals in the barbecue and let burn until the flames have died and the coals are glowing, which should take 30 to 40 minutes. Spread the coals out.

Put the seafood on the oiled grill or tray and cook for 2 to 3 minutes a side; it does not have to be thoroughly cooked since it can finish cooking in the soup, but it should pick up color and flavor from the grilling. If the pieces are large, cut them into bite-sized chunks.

Heat the vegetable oil in a large saucepan. Add the salsa and fry it for 5 minutes. Add the clam juice or seafood stock and the herbs.

Bring to a boil, then reduce the heat and simmer, partially covered, for 15 minutes. Remove the cover and add the onion, bell pepper, and chilies. Simmer for 3 to 4 minutes longer. Add the seafood and cook for 1 to 2 minutes. Add salt and pepper to taste.

Coconut and Shrimp Soup

SERVES 4

1 red bell pepper, cored, seeded, and diced

1½ tbsp chopped scallion including a small amount of green top

2 cups chicken stock

2 tsp chopped garlic

1 tbsp grated gingerroot

1 tbsp ground coriander

½ tbsp curry powder

½ tsp thyme

½ tsp ground white pepper

½ tsp hot pepper sauce

1¼ cups coconut milk (page 14)

1¼ lb shrimp, shelled and deveined

1 cup heavy cream

Mix the bell pepper and scallion together in a bowl and set aside.

Bring the chicken stock, garlic, ginger, coriander, curry powder, thyme, pepper, hot pepper sauce, and coconut milk to a boil in a large saucepan over medium-high heat. Reduce the heat immediately and simmer for about 5 minutes.

Remove the pan from the heat and skim any fat off the top. Return to medium-high heat and bring to a simmer, then add half the pepper and scallion mixture and the shrimp. Simmer just until the shrimp are cooked, about 5 minutes; do not overcook.

Remove the pan from the heat and add the cream. Taste and adjust the seasoning. Ladle into bowls and garnish with the remaining pepper and scallion mixture.

SPICY CHICKEN SOUP

SERVES 4

The leftover chicken from this recipe is ideal to use in **Chicken and Rice Croquettes.**

1 onion, halved

2 celery sticks, including leaves, diced

2 carrots, diced

1 parsnip, diced

5 cloves garlic, peeled

3 lb chicken

5 cups water

½ tsp minced fresh basil

½ tsp curry powder

dash of hot pepper sauce

1 tsp minced fresh coriander

salt and freshly ground black pepper

Divide the vegetables into 2 portions and place in 2 bowls or on sheets of waxed paper.

Place the garlic, chicken and half the vegetables in a saucepan. Add water to cover the chicken, then add the basil, curry powder, hot pepper sauce, coriander and salt and pepper to taste. Bring to a boil, then immediately reduce heat and simmer, uncovered, for about 2 hours.

Skim the fat off the top of the soup, then strain it; refrigerate the cooked chicken for later use.

Add the remaining vegetables. Simmer for another 10 minutes, or until the vegetables are tender. Serve.

PINEAPPLE AND MANGO BISQUE

SERVES 4

3 tbsp sugar

2 tbsp dark rum

2 tbsp water

3 lb pineapple, peeled, cored, and cut into 1-in pieces

2 mangoes, peeled, seeded, and cut into ½-in pieces

3 cups well-chilled milk

pinch of ground cinnamon

½ cup chilled heavy cream, plus more for serving

Put the sugar, rum, and water in a saucepan and bring to a boil over high heat until reduced slightly, 1 to 2 minutes. Remove the pan from the heat and set aside to let the mixture cool.

Combine the pineapple, mangoes, rum syrup, and ½ cup milk in a blender or food processor and purée until smooth.

Strain through a coarse strainer set over a large glass bowl. Beat in the remaining milk, the cinnamon, and the cream. Cover and refrigerate until well chilled, for between 4 to 24 hours.

ICED PASSION FRUIT SOUP WITH YOGURT AND VANILLA

SERVES 4

Look for passion fruits that are large and heavy with dimpled skin and purple in color.

20 fresh passion fruits
½ cup sugar
4-in piece of vanilla bean, split
  lengthwise
1 cup water

2 tsp unflavored gelatin
½ cup plain yogurt, beaten well
fresh mint leaves to garnish
  (optional)

Place a coarse strainer over a medium non-reactive saucepan. Working over the strainer, cut each passion fruit in half and scoop out the pulp with a teaspoon. Push the pulp and juice through the strainer, than discard the seeds.

Add the sugar, vanilla bean, and water to the pan and bring to a simmer over low heat, stirring constantly.

Remove the pan from the heat and sprinkle the gelatin evenly over the mixture, then set aside, undisturbed, for about 3 minutes to let the gelatin thicken on the surface of the juice. Then whisk the mixture well to incorporate the gelatin.

Set a fine strainer over a medium non-reactive bowl and strain the mixture. Leave to cool to room temperature, then place the bowl in a larger bowl filled with ice and water. Chill the mixture over the ice, stirring frequently. (The recipe can be prepared to this point and refrigerated overnight, covered.)

To serve, ladle the chilled soup into 4 shallow soup dishes. Top each serving with 2 tablespoons yogurt and top with mint leaves if desired.

Seafood and Fish Dishes

LOBSTER IN CHILI SAUCE

FRIED FLYING FISH

BAKED LOBSTER

POACHED MARINATED FISH

BRAISED MARINATED FISH, CREOLE STYLE

PIQUANT SHRIMP

CURRIED BAKED ROUGHY

CRABS IN PEPPER SAUCE

CRAB GUMBO

BARBECUED CHILI SHRIMP

SHRIMP SKEWERS

SPICY ISLAND SNAPPER

SHRIMP-STUFFED EDAM CHEESE

SPICY SHARK KEBABS

SHRIMP CREOLE

CALYPSO COD STEAKS

TROPICAL SHRIMP AND LOBSTER SALAD

SNAPPER WITH TOMATO COULIS

BAKED FISH WITH ONIONS

CITRUS-CRUSTED SHRIMP WITH GINGER, STAR FRUIT, AND RUM

TROPICAL SAUTEED SNAPPER

PECAN-ENCRUSTED FLOUNDER

CRAB CAKES

CRAB-STUFFED ZUCCHINI

FISH TIPS

The Caribbean waters are rich in fish and seafood. Typical Caribbean fish are grouper, kingfish, Spanish mackerel, snappers, flying fish (a fish with "wings" that are, in fact, extended fins, found off the coasts of Barbados), and dolphin fish—no relation to the mammal.

✦ Some Caribbean fish have bizarre shapes: the coffer fish, for example, is square-shaped and the moonfish is round and silvery. The people of Martinique have named a fish "bon-die marie moin," which is Creole meaning "good God handled me," for this fish has unearthly fingerprints along its sides.

✦ The Caribbean waters also contain plenty of crabs, shrimp, octopus, spiny lobsters, conch (called lambi), which are enormous sea snails with big horns, and sea eggs, a kind of white sea urchin without spines.

✦ When you buy fish, make sure that it is fresh. Signs of this are eyes that are clear and bright (avoid those with sunken eyes), skin that is shiny and moist, flesh that is firm, and a sea-fresh smell. Frozen fish should be frozen hard, with no sign of partial thawing.

✦ When buying shellfish, make sure the shells are undamaged, without any cracks.

LOBSTER IN CHILI SAUCE

SERVES 2

2 x 2-lb uncooked lobsters, split in half lengthwise
2 tbsp vegetable oil mixed with 1 tsp liquid annatto (page 12)
1¼ cups dry white wine
1 tsp salt
½ chili pepper, finely chopped

Remove and discard the gelatinous sac in the head of each lobster and the long intestinal vein attached to it. Chop off the tail section of each lobster at the point where it joins the body. Twist off the claws and smash the flat side of each claw with a large, heavy knife. Cut off and discard the small claws and antennae.

Heat the oil in a large skillet. Add the lobster bodies, tails, and large claws and fry them, stirring constantly, until the shells turn pink. Transfer the lobsters to a large plate.

Add the wine to the skillet and bring it to a boil. Stir in the salt and chili pepper. Return the lobsters to the pan, coat them evenly in the liquid, and simmer for 10 minutes, basting them from time to time.

To serve, arrange the lobster pieces in a large, heated dish and spoon the sauce over them.

FRIED FLYING FISH

SERVES 6

6 small, boned flying fish
1 tbsp lime or lemon juice
1 garlic clove, crushed
salt and freshly ground black
  pepper

1 tsp chopped fresh thyme
2 whole cloves
2 tsp all-purpose flour
vegetable oil for frying

Marinate the fish in the lemon or lime juice, garlic, salt and freshly ground black pepper, thyme, and cloves for at least 1 hour.

Remove the fish from the marinade and dry them well with paper towels.

Mix the flour with freshly ground black pepper, then coat the fish in it, shaking off any excess.

Heat some oil (enough to cover the fish) in a large skillet. Fry the fish until they are golden brown, then serve. Serve hot with rice and peas, salad, and hot pepper sauce.

BAKED LOBSTER

SERVES 4

2 lb cooked lobster meat, cubed
2 tsp salt
1 garlic clove, crushed
¼ tsp grated nutmeg
freshly ground black pepper
¼ cup butter or margarine

3¾ cups light cream or
  evaporated milk
1 tsp hot pepper sauce
½ small onion, finely chopped
2 egg yolks
1½ cups grated cheese

Put the lobster into a bowl and stir in the salt, garlic, nutmeg, and freshly ground black pepper. Chill it for 1 hour.

Preheat the oven to 350°F.

Melt the butter or margarine in a large saucepan over low heat. Gradually add the cream or evaporated milk, stirring all the time. Add the lobster, hot pepper sauce, and onion, mixing them in well. Beat the egg yolks slightly, then add them to the saucepan.

Spoon the lobster mixture into a greased baking dish. Sprinkle half the grated cheese over the top and bake for 5 minutes.

Sprinkle with the remaining cheese just before serving. Serve on a bed of rice or with mashed sweet potatoes.

POACHED MARINATED FISH

SERVES 2

5 cups water

6 tbsp fresh lime or lemon juice

2 tsp salt

2 x 1-lb fish, scaled, cleaned,
  and cut into four
steaks about 1 in thick (snapper,
  sea bream, or mullet)

1 small onion, finely chopped

1 tsp crushed garlic cloves

1 chili pepper, chopped

2 bay leaves

½ tsp dried thyme

2 scallions, chopped

2 sprigs fresh thyme

Put half the water, half the lime or lemon juice, and salt into a large, shallow, glass baking dish. Wash the fish steaks under cold running water, then put them in the baking dish and leave to marinate for about 1 hour.

Drain and discard the marinade.

Pour the remaining water into a skillet with the onion, garlic, hot pepper, bay leaves, and thyme. Bring to a boil over high heat, then lower the heat and simmer for 5 minutes.

Add the fish steaks to the pan and bring back to a boil. Reduce the heat to the lowest setting, cover the pan, and simmer for 10 minutes, or until the fish flakes easily when tested with the tip of a knife.

Transfer the fish to a warmed serving dish. Add the remaining lime or lemon juice to the cooking liquid, then pour this over the fish. Taste to check the seasoning, then serve at once, garnished with fresh thyme and chopped scallions. Serve with fresh bread.

BRAISED MARINATED FISH, CREOLE STYLE

SERVES 4

2½ cups water

6 tbsp fresh lime or lemon juice

2 tsp salt

2 lb firm fish (such as snapper or mullet), scaled, cleaned, and cut into 4 x ½-lb steaks

3 tbsp vegetable oil mixed with 1 tsp liquid annatto (see page 12)

4 scallions, chopped

4 garlic cloves, chopped

½ chili pepper, finely chopped

3 tomatoes, skinned and chopped

1 tsp fresh thyme

1 bay leaf

4 parsley sprigs

freshly ground black pepper

2 tbsp olive oil

Put 2 cups water, the lime or lemon juice and salt into a large, shallow, glass dish, and stir until the salt dissolves. Rinse the fish steaks under cold running water. Marinate in the lime or lemon juice mixture for 1 hour.

Remove the fish from the marinade. Heat the annatto-flavored oil in a large saucepan over medium heat. Add the scallions, garlic, and hot pepper and fry until soft.

Add the tomatoes, thyme, bay leaf, parsley, and freshly ground black pepper and simmer for 10 minutes.

Stir in the remaining water. Add the fish and bring to a boil, then reduce the heat and simmer for 10 minutes longer.

Transfer the fish and sauce to a heated baking dish. Sprinkle with the olive oil and bake for 5 minutes.

PIQUANT SHRIMP

SERVES 4 TO 6

1 cup unsalted butter

½ cup olive oil

3 scallions, chopped

6 cloves garlic, finely chopped

1 tbsp chopped fresh basil

1½ tsp fresh oregano

1 tsp dried red-pepper flakes

1 tsp paprika

1 tsp salt

1 tbsp fresh lemon juice

2 lb medium or large shrimp, shelled and deveined

Preheat the oven to 450°F.

To make the sauce, melt butter, then mix with all ingredients, except the shrimp; the sauce may be made a day in advance and refrigerated. (If you make the sauce in advance, you don't need to melt the butter or mix ingredients well. When you are ready to cook the shrimp, melt the whole mixture and blend well.)

Spread the shrimp in a 9- x 13-inch baking pan or other wide, shallow baking dish. Pour the sauce over the shrimp. Turn the shrimp so the sauce coats them all.

Bake for 5 to 10 minutes until the shrimp curl tightly, lose their translucence, and turn white. You may need to turn the shrimp once or twice during cooking to be sure they cook evenly.

CURRIED BAKED ROUGHY

SERVES 4

Roughy is a mild-flavored, usually inexpensive, lean white fish that lends itself to many assertive sauces. If you can't find roughy, use red snapper, turbot, sole, grouper, halibut, or haddock.

vegetable oil
4 x 4-oz orange roughy fillets
½ cup mayonnaise
2 tbsp dry white wine
2 tbsp lime or lemon juice
1 tsp dried dill
1 tsp curry powder

Preheat the oven to 350°F. Brush a grill rack with vegetable oil. Place the rack in a shallow baking pan and arrange the fillets on the rack.

Combine the mayonnaise, wine, lime or lemon juice, dill, and curry powder in a bowl and blend together well.

Spread the curry mixture evenly over the fillets. Bake for 25 minutes, or until the fish flakes easily when tested with a fork.

CRABS IN PEPPER SAUCE

SERVES 6

3 tbsp olive oil
1 chili pepper, finely chopped
1 onion, finely chopped
½ green bell pepper, cored, seeded, and finely chopped
2 garlic cloves, finely chopped
6 tomatoes, skinned and chopped
3 tbsp tomato paste
1 tsp salt
freshly ground black pepper
1 lb fresh, canned, or frozen crabmeat
2 tbsp fresh lime or lemon juice
2 tbsp finely chopped fresh coriander

Heat the oil in a large skillet over medium heat. Add the hot pepper, onion, green pepper, and garlic and fry for 5 minutes, stirring frequently.

Add the tomatoes, tomato paste, salt, and freshly ground black pepper to taste. Bring the mixture to a boil, then lower the heat and cook, uncovered, until it has reduced to a thick sauce.

Add the crabmeat and stir it in. Simmer for 2 minutes. Serve sprinkled with the lime or lemon juice and chopped coriander.

CRAB GUMBO

SERVES 6

2 x 2-lb cooked crabs
2 tbsp butter or margarine
1 tbsp vegetable oil
1 onion, chopped
14-oz can tomatoes, drained
   and chopped
1 tbsp chopped fresh thyme

2 tbsp chopped fresh parsley
½ lb okra, trimmed and sliced
1 fresh chili pepper
2½ cups boiling water
salt and freshly ground black
   pepper

Cut the legs and claws off the crabs, and crack them using a nutcracker. Cut the body into quarters.

Heat the butter or margarine and oil in a large saucepan over medium heat. Add the onion and fry for 5 minutes. Add the crabs and simmer, turning frequently.

Stir in the tomatoes, thyme, and parsley, and cook for 5 minutes longer.

Add the okra and chili pepper, and pour in 2½ cups boiling water. Season with salt and freshly ground black pepper, then lower the heat and continue simmering for 45 minutes.

Discard the chili pepper, and spoon the stew into warmed soup bowls. Serve with fresh bread.

BARBECUED CHILI SHRIMP

SERVES 4

1 lb raw jumbo shrimp, thawed
  if frozen
salad leaves and lime twists to
  garnish

FOR THE MARINADE

grated peel and juice of 2 limes

3 chili peppers, seeded and
  sliced
2-in piece fresh gingerroot,
  peeled and grated
2 garlic cloves, crushed
1 tbsp honey, warmed
6 tbsp olive oil
1 tbsp freshly chopped cilantro

If using fresh shrimp, shell and devein them. Place them in a shallow dish.

Mix the marinade ingredients together and pour over the shrimp. Cover and leave to marinate for at least 4 hours, turning occasionally in the marinade.

Meanwhile, soak 4 long wooden skewers in cold water for 1 hour. Light the barbecue coals 20 minutes before required, or preheat the broiler to medium-hot. Drain the shrimp and reserve a little of the marinade. Thread the shrimp onto the skewers and brush with the marinade.

Barbecue or broil, turning at least once, for 5 minutes, or until the shrimp turn pink. Serve garnished with salad leaves and lime twists.

SHRIMP SKEWERS

*1 lb medium to large shrimp,
    shelled and deveined*
½ cup olive oil
3 cloves garlic, minced

3 tbsp fresh lime juice
2 tbsp chopped fresh basil
1 tsp red-pepper flakes

Place the shrimp in a glass or plastic bowl. Mix together all the remaining ingredients. Pour this marinade over the shrimp and stir, making sure that all the shrimp are thoroughly coated. Marinate, refrigerated, for 2 to 4 hours, stirring 2 or 3 times.

About 45 minutes before you want to eat, start the barbecue fire. If you plan to use wooden skewers, soak them in water for at least 30 minutes so they don't burn easily. A few minutes before the coals are ready, thread the shrimp loosely on the skewers. If they are crammed together, they will not cook evenly.

When the flames have died down and the coals are glowing and covered with white ash, place the shrimp on the greased broiler rack. They will cook quickly, especially if dripping marinade causes flare-ups, so they need to be closely watched.

Broil for 2 to 4 minutes, turning once, until cooked through, depending on the size of the shrimp and the distance from the coals. The shrimp will lose their translucency and turn an opaque white-pink. Do not overcook them, or they will get tough.

Serve with salsas of your choice.

SPICY ISLAND SNAPPER

*4 fillets of red snapper, about
    6 oz each*
salt and pepper
4 tbsp all-purpose flour
2 tbsp vegetable oil
*1½ cups Broiled Tomato Salsa
    (page 138)*

*½ red bell pepper, cored, seeded,
    and cut into strips*
*1 or 2 jalapeño chilies, seeded
    and cut into rings*
¼ cup chopped scallion
1 tbsp chopped fresh cilantro

Season the fish fillets with salt and pepper, then dust with the flour.

Heat the oil in a skillet. Add the fillets and cook them quickly so that each side is lightly browned.

Add the salsa, red pepper, and chilies to the pan. Simmer over low heat, spooning the salsa over the fish. Continue simmering until the fish flakes easily.

Put the fish onto serving plates, spooning salsa, red pepper strips, and chili rings over each piece. Garnish with the scallions and cilantro.

SHRIMP-STUFFED EDAM CHEESE

SERVES 6

4-lb whole Edam cheese

¼ cup butter or margarine

2 tsp vegetable oil

1 tbsp finely chopped onion

1 tomato, skinned and chopped

¼ tsp chili powder

½ tsp salt

freshly ground black pepper

¼ lb cooked shrimp, shelled, deveined, and chopped

3 tbsp fresh, white bread crumbs

1 egg, well beaten

2 tbsp raisins

Peel the wax off the cheese, and cut a 1-inch thick slice off the top and reserve. Scoop out the center of the cheese with a spoon to leave a shell 1 inch thick, reserving the scooped out cheese.

Place both the shell and top in enough cold water to cover them, and leave them to soak for 1 hour.

Remove the cheese shell and top from the water, turn upside down, and leave them on paper towels to drain.

Grate the cheese removed from the center.

Preheat the oven to 350°F.

Grease a round baking dish with half the butter or margarine; it has to be large enough to hold the cheese shell—not too shallow or too large, but about the same size as the cheese shell itself.

Heat the remaining butter or margarine and vegetable oil in a skillet over medium heat. Add the onion and cook for 5 minutes without letting it turn.

Add the tomato, chili powder, salt, and a few grindings of black pepper. Continue to cook until the mixture becomes thick, then transfer it to a bowl.

Add the grated cheese, shrimp, bread crumbs, egg, and raisins.

Spoon the mixture into the cheese shell, cover with the cheese top, and put it in the prepared baking dish. Bake, uncovered, for 30 minutes until the top has browned slightly. Serve at once, straight from the baking dish.

MARINE ISLAND CACTUS, ST. LUCIA.

SPICY SHARK KEBABS

SERVES 4

Sword fish, or any other firm fish, is a delicious substitute for the shark.

2 cloves garlic, crushed

½ cup olive oil, divided

1½ lb shark steak, cut into kebab-sized cubes

2 tbsp fresh lime juice

2 tbsp ground cumin

2 tbsp paprika

1 tsp cayenne

2 tsp freshly ground black pepper

1 small eggplant, cubed

1 zucchini, cut into ½-in slices

16 mushrooms

1 onion, cut into chunks

1 green or red bell pepper, cored, seeded, and cut into chunks

If you are using wooden skewers, soak them in water for at least 30 minutes so they don't catch fire. Ignite barbecue coals about 30 minutes before you want to begin broiling.

Mix the garlic cloves with ¼ cup olive oil; set aside, letting the garlic flavor the oil. (Or, if you have a microwave, crush 2 garlic cloves with flat side of knife. Put the oil and garlic into a small bowl. Microwave on 50% power for 5 minutes until the garlic is lightly browned.) Set the oil aside, letting the garlic steep.

Put the cubes of shark in a glass bowl. Mix remaining ¼ cup olive oil with lime juice, then pour it over the shark. Toss the shark meat so all the cubes are covered with the oil. Let the meat marinate about 20 minutes.

Drain the fish. Combine the cumin, paprika, cayenne, and black pepper. Sprinkle about two-thirds of the spice mixture over the shark and toss so that all cubes are seasoned.

While fish is marinating, prepare vegetables. Place the eggplant, zucchini, and mushrooms in a glass bowl. Discard the garlic from the olive oil, pour the oil over the vegetables and toss quickly to spread the oil evenly, since the vegetables soak up liquids like sponges. Sprinkle the remaining spice mix over the vegetables, and toss again.

Thread the shark, seasoned vegetables, onion and pepper onto skewers; do not press the pieces too tightly together, as they will not cook evenly.

Lightly oil the barbecue rack. When coals are white and no longer flaming, place the skewers on the rack over the coals. Turn once or twice and barbecue for about 10 minutes for each inch of thickness until fish is flaky and loses its translucency.

SHRIMP CREOLE

SERVES 4 – 6

2 tbsp vegetable oil

1 large onion, chopped

8 cloves garlic, minced

2 large celery sticks, finely
  chopped

4 tomatoes, chopped

2 green bell peppers, cored,
  seeded, and chopped

2 tbsp tomato paste

1 tsp hot pepper sauce

½ tsp dried oregano

1 tsp dried thyme

2 tsp Worcestershire sauce

5 cups chicken stock

1½ lb shrimp, shelled and
  deveined

8-oz can sliced water chestnuts,
  drained and rinsed, or 8 oz
  jicama, sliced

½ tbsp lime juice

salt and freshly ground black
  pepper

4 cups cooked white long-grain
  rice

1 tbsp minced coriander or
  parsley to garnish

Heat the oil in a large saucepan, skillet, or wok. Add the onion, garlic, celery, tomatoes, and peppers and fry over medium heat until tender.

Add the tomato paste, hot pepper sauce, oregano, and thyme and blend, stirring constantly, for about 2 minutes. Add the Worcestershire sauce and chicken stock and bring to a boil over medium-high heat for about 30 minutes until thickened.

Add the shrimp and water chestnuts and simmer for about 4 minutes, uncovered, until the shrimp are opaque.

Remove the pan from the heat and adjust the seasoning with more hot pepper sauce to taste, lime juice, and salt and pepper.

Serve over or under a scoop of rice on warm dishes and sprinkle the top with coriander or parsley.

Serve immediately.

CALYPSO COD STEAKS

SERVES 6

3 tbsp fresh lime juice

2 tbsp olive oil

2 tsp minced garlic

2 tsp hot pepper sauce (page 109)

6 cod or salmon steaks, ¾ in thick and weighing about 6 oz each

Beat together the lime juice, olive oil, garlic, and hot pepper sauce in a glass bowl.

Brush the broiler rack with oil and preheat the broiler.

Broil the steaks for 10 to 12 minutes on one side, basting frequently with the sauce. Turn and cook on the other side for another 10 to 12 minutes, again basting frequently, until done but not overcooked.

SHRIMP TAMARINDO

SERVES 4

2 tbsp butter or margarine

2 tbsp minced onion

1 clove garlic, crushed

1 green bell pepper, cored, seeded, and chopped

2 tbsp tomato paste

¼ cup sherry

1 bay leaf

½ cup tamarind juice (page 17)

2 tbsp honey

¼ tsp ground allspice

¼ tsp salt

⅛ tsp hot pepper sauce

1 lb raw jumbo shrimp, shelled and deveined

1 tbsp fresh lime or lemon juice

Melt the butter in a large skillet. Add the onion, garlic, and green pepper and fry until tender, stirring frequently. Add the tomato paste, sherry, bay leaf, tamarind juice, honey, allspice, and salt, stirring constantly, until heated through.

Reduce the heat and simmer about 5 minutes, uncovered, until slightly thickened. Add hot pepper sauce to taste.

Add the shrimp and stir for 3 to 5 minutes until they turn pink. Remove the bay leaf and stir in the lime or lemon juice. Serve on a bed of steamed rice.

TROPICAL SHRIMP AND LOBSTER SALAD

SERVES 4

1 lb cooked shrimp, shelled and
    deveined
2 x 5-oz cans lobster, drained
    and broken into ½-in pieces
1 fresh mango, cubed
1 green bell pepper, cored,
    seeded and thinly sliced
½ onion, thinly sliced
1 cup thinly sliced celery
1½ cups cubed fresh pineapple

½ cup plain yogurt
½ cup sour cream
½ cup fresh orange juice
4 tsp fresh lime juice
2 tsp grated fresh gingerroot

FOR THE GARNISH

lettuce leaves (optional)
crescent slices of mango

Combine the shrimp, lobster, mango, green pepper, onion, celery, and pineapple in a bowl, then cover and chill.

Beat together the yogurt, sour cream, orange juice, lime juice, and ginger.

To serve, gently toss together the chilled shrimp, lobster, fruits and vegetables. Pour the dressing over the salad and toss together. Serve over lettuce leaves, if desired, and garnish with a crescent of mango slices.

SNAPPER WITH TOMATO COULIS

SERVES 4

2 large red mullet or snappers,
    filleted and boned
4 tbsp olive oil
½ cup lime juice
2 green chili peppers, seeded and
    finely sliced
1 to 2 tsp honey, warmed

FOR THE TOMATO COULIS

1 tbsp olive oil
2 shallots, chopped

1 garlic clove, crushed
3 red chili peppers, seeded and
    chopped
1 tbsp tomato paste
1 tbsp water
3 cups peeled, seeded, and
    chopped tomatoes
juice of ½ lemon
salt and freshly ground black
    pepper
lime wedges and grated lime
    peel to garnish

Rinse the fish and pat it dry with paper towels. Place in a shallow dish. Mix the oil, lime juice, chilies, and honey together and pour over the fish. Cover and leave to marinate for at least 1 hour, turning the fish occasionally during this time.

Meanwhile, make the tomato coulis. Heat the oil in a pan. Add the shallots, garlic, and chilies and fry for 5 minutes, or until softened. Blend the tomato paste with the water and add to the pan with the chopped tomatoes, lime juice, and seasonings.

Bring to a boil, cover the pan, reduce the heat, and simmer for 15 minutes.

Remove the pan from the heat and let the mixture cool slightly. Place in a blender or food processor and purée, then pass through a fine strainer to remove any seeds. Check the seasoning and heat gently when required.

Preheat the broiler to medium and line the broiler rack with foil. Drain the fish and place on the foil-lined rack. Broil for 8 to 10 minutes, turning the fish over once, or until tender and the flesh flakes easily.

To serve, pour the tomato coulis onto 4 serving plates and place the cooked fish on top. Garnish with lime wedges and grated lime peel or perhaps watercress.

BAKED FISH WITH ONIONS

SERVES 6

2 lb red snappers or similar fish

salt and freshly ground black
  pepper

2 garlic cloves, crushed

juice of 1 lemon

1 cup water

1 large onion, finely chopped

6 tbsp fresh bread crumbs

½ cup olive oil

1 tbsp chopped fresh parsley

Clean, wash, and prepare the fish. Make an incision along the belly of each fish. Lightly sprinkle salt and freshly ground black pepper and some garlic both inside and outside. Rub lemon juice over the fish. Place in a pan, pour the water over the fish, and leave to marinate for at least 1 hour, preferably 4.

Preheat the oven to 350°F.

Cook half the onion, the remaining garlic, and half the bread crumbs in 1 tablespoon of the oil. Add a little water to make the mixture form a slightly crumbly texture, then leave it to cool.

Stuff the fish with the onion and bread crumbs mixture, then lay them in a greased baking dish and cover with the rest of the oil. Sprinkle the rest of the onion and bread crumbs and the parsley over them.

Bake them in the preheated oven for 30 minutes.

CITRUS-CRUSTED SHRIMP WITH
GINGER, STAR FRUIT, AND RUM

SERVES 4

This dish was created by Allen Susser of Chef Allen's, Miami. If you don't like the flavor of rum, substitute fresh lime juice.

grated peel and juice of 2 lemons
grated peel and juice of 2 limes
1 chili pepper, seeded and diced
1 tbsp white peppercorns,
  crushed
1 tbsp kosher salt
2 tbsp brown sugar

1 tbsp olive oil
12 raw jumbo shrimp, shelled,
  deveined, and butterflied
vegetable oil for sautéeing
2 star fruit, sliced crosswise
2 tsp sliced fresh gingerroot
4 tbsp rum or lime juice

Combine lime and lemon peels, chili pepper, and peppercorns and set aside.

Simmer the lemon and lime juices and brown sugar in a small saucepan until 3 tablespoons are left. Add salt and peel mixture. Cook for 1 minute longer, then remove from heat. Moisten with 1 tablespoon oil and let cool.

Press mixture onto both sides of butterflied shrimp. Heat the remaining oil in a large skillet. Add the shrimp and cook for 1 minute, then add star fruit and ginger. Add rum, swirl it around in pan for a few seconds, and serve immediately.

TROPICAL SAUTÉED SNAPPER

SERVES 4

Place this noble fish on a bed of Mangolade. For a finishing touch, top the fish with Pineapple-Coconut Salsa (page 138).

If you can't find snapper, substitute any white, firm-fleshed fish, such as perch, turbot or sole.

4 snapper fillets, 6 to 8 oz each

all-purpose flour

salt and freshly ground white pepper

FOR THE TANGO MANGO BUTTER LOG

1 cup butter, softened

1 cup puréed canned mango

2 tsp freshly squeezed lime juice

2 tbsp finely chopped fresh mint

1 tsp grated nutmeg

FOR THE MANGOLADE

1 cup mango chutney, chopped

1 cup orange marmalade

½ cup whole-grain mustard

1 tbsp horseradish

First make the butter log. Beat all the ingredients together, then roll into a log shape. Wrap in waxed paper and freeze until required. To make the Mangolade, combine the chutney, marmalade, mustard and horseradish in a bowl. Cover and chill until ready to serve.

Lightly dust the snapper fillets with flour. Add salt and white pepper to taste.

Melt butter log in a large skillet over medium-high heat. Place fillets into pan and sauté until lightly browned on both sides. Drain well on paper towels and serve at once accompanied by the Mangolade.

PECAN-ENCRUSTED FLOUNDER

SERVES 4

salt and freshly ground pepper

8 small flounder fillets, about
  8 oz total, skinned

1 large egg

3 tbsp water

2 tsp dark soy sauce

¼ cup finely chopped pecans

3 tbsp vegetable oil

2 tbsp olive oil (optional)

3 tbsp chopped fresh coriander
  or parsley for garnish
  (optional)

2 tbsp Tango Mango Butter Log
  (page 77)

butter or margarine (optional)

1 tbsp freshly squeezed lime
  juice (optional)

Salt and pepper both sides of fillets. Beat the egg, water and soy sauce together in a large bowl. Dip fillets, one at a time, in the egg mixture to coat lightly, then dredge evenly in nuts.

Heat 1 tablespoon of the vegetable oil in a large nonstick skillet, When hot, add as many fillets as will fit without crowding and sauté for a total of about 2 minutes, or until lightly browned on both sides; add more oil, if needed. Garnish and serve fillets.

If you wish to serve the butter over the fillets, transfer fillets to a warm serving plate or platter and wipe the skillet with paper towels. Add remaining olive oil and Tango-Mango Butter and cook until the butter foams and starts to brown. Add lime juice, stir once, and then pour mixture over fish. Garnish, and serve.

CRAB CAKES

SERVES 4

1 lb lump crabmeat

5 salted crackers, crumbled in
   blender

2 eggs, beaten

½ cup finely chopped fresh
   parsley

1 tsp Worcestershire sauce

2 to 3 tbsp mayonnaise and/or
   Dijon mustard

vegetable oil for frying

clarified butter or ghee or frying

salt and freshly ground pepper

Remove any shell or cartilage from crabmeat. Mix all ingredients, except the butter or oil, together gently but thoroughly with a fork. Refrigerate for at least 1 hour for easier handling, then mold into patties.

Place a thin layer of clarified butter or ghee in the bottom of a skillet large enough to hold all 4 patties one-layer deep. Heat over medium-high heat until sizzling hot.

Add the patties and fry until golden brown on one side, and then turn over with a pancake turner and fry until golden brown on other side.

Remove the crab cakes from the pan and drain on paper towels. Serve immediately.

CRAB-STUFFED ZUCCHINI

SERVES 4 OR 8

4 thick zucchini

3 tbsp vegetable oil

¾ cup chopped onion

¾ cup chopped celery

⅓ cup finely chopped seeded
   green bell pepper

2 cloves garlic, finely chopped

¾ cup dry bread crumbs

1 tsp dried basil

½ tsp dried thyme

1 tsp salt

¼ tsp black pepper

¼ tsp cayenne pepper

2 to 3 tbsp milk or clam juice

12 oz fresh crabmeat

Parmesan cheese

Preheat oven to 350°F. Lightly grease a large, shallow baking dish.

Cut the zucchini in half lengthwise. Scoop out the pulp, leaving a ¼-inch shell and chop the pulp.

Heat the oil in a large skillet. Add the onion, celery, green pepper, and garlic and fry for 10–12 minutes, stirring frequently, until the vegetables are tender and excess moisture has evaporated. Remove vegetables from heat.

Meanwhile, preheat the oven to 350°F.

Mix the bread crumbs, herbs and spices, and cooked vegetables together in a large bowl. Add enough milk or clam juice so that the mixture is moist, but not mushy.

With your fingers, pick through the crabmeat to remove any bits of bone or cartilage. Gently mix it into the stuffing.

Mound the stuffing into zucchini shells. Sprinkle with Parmesan cheese. Place the zucchini in the baking dish. Bake for about 20 minutes until the zucchini are tender. Serve immediately.

Chicken Dishes

CARIB-ORIENT CHICKEN

CALYPSO CHICKEN

GRILLED CHICKEN WITH SALSA

CHICKEN AND RICE STEW

ROAST CHICKEN, HAITI STYLE

CITRUS-FRIED CHICKEN

CORIANDER CHICKEN

SWEET-AND-SPICY CHICKEN

JERK MON'S CHICKEN

STEWED CHICKEN, TRINIDAD STYLE

CHICKEN WITH RICE AND PIGEON PEAS

CARIB-ORIENT CHICKEN

SERVES 4

3-lb chicken, boned and cut into
  2-in pieces
½ cup soy sauce
2 tbsp brown sugar

2 garlic cloves, crushed
1 tbsp grated fresh gingerroot
3 tbsp white wine

Rinse the chicken pieces and put them in a bowl.

Combine the remaining ingredients in a large saucepan and stir over medium heat until the sugar dissolves. Leave to cool.

Pour the sauce over the chicken and leave to marinate for 5 hours.

When ready to serve, preheat the broiler. Broil the chicken pieces until they are tender and cooked through and serve.

CALYPSO CHICKEN

SERVES 6

3-lb chicken, boned and cut into
  2-in pieces
½ lemon
2 tsp salt
freshly ground black pepper
2 garlic cloves
1 tbsp vinegar
¼ tsp chopped fresh thyme

2 tbsp butter or margarine
2 tsp brown sugar
oil for frying
1 cup cashew nuts
1¼ cups sliced mushrooms
3 onions, chopped
6 slices fresh gingerroot
1 tbsp all-purpose flour

Rinse the chicken in cold running water, rubbing with the lemon. Season with the salt, pepper, one of the cloves of garlic, crushed, plus the vinegar, and thyme. Leave to marinate for about 3 hours.

Melt the butter or margarine in a large saucepan. Add the sugar. When it is bubbling, add the chicken and brown the pieces.

Meanwhile, heat some oil in a skillet. Fry half the cashews, then set them aside.

In the same pan, fry together the remaining clove of garlic, crushed, the mushrooms, the other half of the cashews, onions, and ginger. Add ¼ cup water and pour into the large saucepan over the chicken. Simmer for 25 minutes, or until the chicken is tender and cooked through.

Thicken the mixture with the flour mixed with some warm water and stir into the chicken mixture. Cook for 3 minutes longer, then sprinkle with the remaining fried cashews. Serve with boiled rice.

GRILLED CHICKEN WITH SALSA

SERVES 4

½ cup olive oil

2 tbsp fresh lime juice

3 tbsp fresh orange juice

2 cloves garlic, minced

1 tbsp chopped fresh cilantro

¼ tsp hot pepper sauce

4 boneless chicken breast halves, with or without skin

1 tsp freshly ground black pepper

½ to 1 cup salsa of your choice

Make a marinade by mixing together all the ingredients, except the chicken, the salsa, and the black pepper. Put the chicken in a glass bowl and pour the marinade over it. Turn the chicken breasts so they are thoroughly coated, then let marinate, refrigerated, for at least 6 hours or overnight; turn the chicken 2 or 3 times while it is marinating.

About 1 hour before serving time, start the fire in the barbecue. When the flames have died, and the coals are glowing and covered with white ash, about 40 minutes, sprinkle the chicken with freshly ground black pepper.

Put the chicken breasts on the greased broiler rack over the coals. Broil, turning once, for about 12 minutes, until the chicken is cooked through and the juices run clear, depending on the thickness of the meat and the distance from the coals. Serve hot or cold or cut into chunks on a bed of green salad.

CHICKEN AND RICE STEW

SERVES 6

1 garlic clove, chopped

½ tsp dried oregano

½ tsp salt

3-lb chicken, boned and cut into 8 pieces

¼ cup butter or margarine

1 small onion, finely chopped

⅔ cup green bell peppers, seeded, and chopped

4 tomatoes, skinned and chopped

1½ cups uncooked long-grain white rice

1¾ quarts chicken stock

freshly ground black pepper

2¼ cups frozen peas

¼ cup freshly grated Parmesan cheese

1 fresh chili pepper, chopped

Mix the garlic, oregano, and salt together in a large bowl. Add the chicken pieces and mix them well together.

Melt the butter or margarine in a saucepan and brown the chicken pieces. Transfer them to a plate.

Add the onion and green peppers to the pan and fry them until they are soft.

Add the tomatoes and browned chicken pieces, coating them well with the onion, peppers, and tomato mixture. Reduce the heat and simmer for 30 minutes, or until the chicken is tender and the juices run clear.

Remove the chicken to a plate and leave to cool a little. Remove the bones, and cut the flesh into 2-inch pieces.

Meanwhile, add the rice, stock, and freshly ground black pepper to the onion, peppers and tomato mixture. Bring to a boil, then reduce the heat, cover, and simmer for 20 minutes, or until the rice is tender.

Stir in the peas, Parmesan, and chili pepper. Mix well, then add the chicken. Cover and simmer for 2 minutes longer, then serve.

ROAST CHICKEN, HAITI STYLE

SERVES 6

½ cup butter or margarine

1 small clove garlic, peeled

6 tbsp soft, fresh bread crumbs

3 tbsp lime juice

2 tsp finely grated lime peel

4 tbsp dark rum

1 tsp brown sugar

¼ tsp ground cinnamon

¼ tsp cayenne pepper

1 tsp salt

freshly ground black pepper

3 ripe bananas

*4 lb whole roasting chicken,
    turkey, or goose*

1¼ cups chicken stock

Preheat oven to 350°F.

First make the stuffing. Melt half the butter or margarine in a small skillet. Add the garlic and stir it around the pan for 10 seconds, then remove and discard the garlic. Add the bread crumbs, two-thirds of the lime juice, the lime peel, a quarter of the rum, the sugar, cinnamon, cayenne pepper, and salt and freshly ground black pepper. Mix well and set on one side.

Peel and chop the bananas, then put them in a bowl. Add the remaining lime juice, 2 tablespoons rum, and salt and freshly ground black pepper. Mix well together.

Stuff the chicken or other fowl with the banana stuffing, and sew the opening closed with a large needle and trussing string.

Fill the small neck cavity with the bread crumb stuffing, then sew up the opening in the same way.

Brush the chicken with the remaining butter or margarine. Place it in a roasting pan and roast for 1 hour, basting occasionally with the juices.

After removing the chicken from the oven, transfer it to a large heated dish and leave to rest for 5 minutes, because this makes it easier to carve.

Meanwhile, skim the fat from the juices left in the roasting pan, and pour in the chicken stock. Bring to a boil over high heat, stirring all the time. Cook for 2 minutes, taste for seasoning, and pour into a sauceboat.

Just before serving, warm the last tablespoon of rum in a small pan. Remove it from the heat, then set light to the rum with a match and pour it, flaming, over the chicken. Serve immediately.

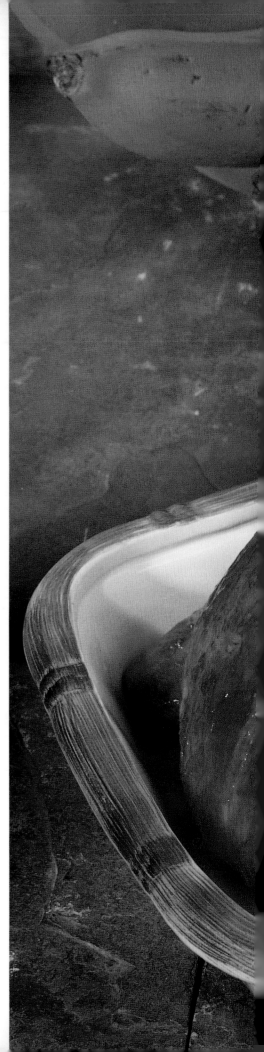

CITRUS-FRIED CHICKEN

SERVES 4

1 chicken, cut up

¼ cup fresh lime juice

¼ cup fresh lemon juice

¼ cup fresh orange juice

¼ cup olive oil

4 garlic cloves, crushed

few drops hot pepper sauce

1 cup all-purpose flour

1 tsp salt

¼ tsp black pepper

vegetable oil or lard

First make the marinade by mixing together the fruit juices, olive oil, garlic, and hot pepper sauce. Trim any excess fat off the chicken and remove skin, if desired. Put the chicken pieces in a glass dish. Pour the marinade over the chicken, making sure that each piece is coated. Marinate in refrigerator for at least 3 hours or overnight.

Combine the flour, salt and pepper in a bowl. Dip each chicken piece in the flour mixture so there is a thin coating of flour over the entire piece; shake off any excess.

Heat ½ to 1 inch oil or lard in a heavy-bottomed skillet until very hot. Carefully place chicken in the hot oil without overcrowding. You probably will need to fry the chicken in two batches (keep the first batch warm in the oven while the second is cooking), or use two skillets. Watch carefully so that the chicken does not burn. Continue cooking for 20 to 25 minutes until the chicken is tender and the juices run clear.

CORIANDER CHICKEN

SERVES 4

3-lb chicken, boned and cut into
  2-in pieces
1 tsp salt
½ tsp freshly ground black
  pepper

3 garlic cloves
2 tsp lemon juice
2 tbsp ground coriander
1 small bunch fresh cilantro
3 tbsp butter or margarine

Season the chicken with the salt, pepper, garlic, lemon juice, and half the ground coriander. Chop the fresh coriander finely and mix it in with the chicken, then leave to marinate for 4 hours.

Preheat the oven to 350°F.

Drain the chicken. Melt the butter or margarine. Place the chicken in a baking dish and pour the melted butter or margarine over it. Sprinkle with the remaining ground coriander, then bake for 1 hour, or until the chicken is tender and the juices run clear.

Just before serving, broil the chicken to brown it. Serve with rice and salad.

SWEET-AND-SPICY CHICKEN

SERVES 6

3-lb chicken, boned and cut into
  2-in pieces
2 tbsp olive oil
1 onion, finely chopped
2 scallions, finely chopped
2 garlic cloves, crushed
1 fresh chili pepper, chopped
½ tsp brown sugar
1 tsp thyme
1 tsp basil

1 christophene, peeled, seeded,
  and chopped
1 eggplant, peeled and cubed
¼ lb okra, trimmed and chopped
14-oz can tomatoes, drained
  and chopped
salt and freshly ground black
  pepper

Rinse the chicken pieces.

Heat the oil in a large saucepan. Add the onion, scallions, and garlic and cook over low heat for 5 minutes. Add the chicken pieces and cook for a further 5 minutes to brown them.

Stir in the chili pepper, sugar, herbs, and vegetables, and season to taste with salt and freshly ground black pepper. Pour in 1¼ cups cold water and bring to a boil, then lower the heat and, stirring occasionally, simmer, uncovered, for 1 hour, or until the chicken and vegetables are cooked and the sauce has thickened. Serve with fresh bread, baked yams, or boiled rice.

JERK MON'S CHICKEN

SERVES 4 TO 6

This jerk dish incorporates a classic rub—a combination of spices, brown sugar, and chili peppers that is applied to the chicken to enliven the dish. Be sure to use the extremely hot *habañero* or Scotch Bonnet chili peppers.

3 tbsp stemmed, seeded, and chopped chili peppers

4 tsp allspice berries, crushed in a pestle and mortar or 1 tsp ground allspice

6 cloves garlic, crushed

2 tbsp peeled and chopped gingerroot

2 tbsp dark brown sugar

3 tbsp yellow mustard

1 tsp ground cinnamon

hot pepper sauce to taste

½ cup olive oil

2 scallions, sliced

¼ cup cider vinegar

2 tbsp lime juice

salt and freshly ground black pepper

3 to 3½ lb chicken, jointed, or 6 large whole legs or 4 large breast halves

Put the chili peppers in a blender or food processor and purée. Add the allspice, garlic, ginger, sugar, mustard, cinnamon, hot pepper sauce, olive oil, scallions, vinegar, and lime juice and blend until the mixture forms a smooth paste. Add salt and pepper to taste and blend again.

Cut the chicken legs and thighs apart. Cut breasts in half crosswise, leaving the wings attached. Gently lift the skin up from the chicken, exposing the meat, and rub the paste underneath. Then rub it into the outside of the skin. Cover with plastic wrap and refrigerate for 2 hours.

To cook on a covered barbecue, place the coals on one side and the chicken on the other. Cover and cook for 40 to 50 minutes until the juices run clear.

To cook in the oven, preheat it to 350°F. Bake the chicken for 50 minutes, then transfer it to the broiler and broil for 2 to 3 minutes on each side until the skin is dark brown and crusty.

STEWED CHICKEN, TRINIDAD STYLE

SERVES 4 TO 6

2 tbsp lime juice

1 onion, chopped

1 large tomato, cut into 8 wedges

1 celery stick, chopped

1 tbsp chopped scallion

3 tbsp minced fresh coriander

1 clove garlic, chopped

⅛ tsp dried thyme, crumbled

1 tsp salt

⅛ tsp freshly ground black pepper

1 tbsp white-wine vinegar

2 tbsp Worcestershire sauce

1½–2 lb chicken, cut into serving pieces

2 tbsp vegetable oil

2 tbsp dark brown sugar

2 tbsp tomato catsup

1 cup water

3 cups shredded cabbage (optional)

celery leaves (optional) to garnish

lime slices (optional) to garnish

Combine the lime juice, onion, tomato, celery, scallion, coriander, garlic, thyme, salt, pepper, vinegar and Worcestershire sauce in a large bowl. Add the chicken, turning it to coat well, and leave it to marinate in the refrigerator, covered, overnight.

Heat the oil in a large saucepan over medium-high heat until it is hot but not smoking. Add the sugar. When the sugar begins to bubble, transfer the chicken in batches to the pan, using a slotted spoon; reserve the marinade mixture. Cook the chicken, turning it until it is browned well, then transfer it to paper towels to drain.

Stir the reserved marinade mixture, tomato catsup, and water into the fat remaining in the saucepan and return the chicken to the pan. Bring the mixture to a boil, then lower the heat and simmer, covered, stirring occasionally, for 30 minutes. Add the shredded cabbage, if using, and simmer for 15 to 20 minutes longer until the thickest pieces of chicken are tender and the juices run clear.

Garnish with celery leaves or lime slices if desired.

CHICKEN WITH RICE AND PIGEON PEAS

SERVES 6

1 onion, chopped

2 garlic cloves

1 tbsp chopped fresh chives

1 tbsp chopped fresh thyme

2 celery sticks with leaves,
    chopped

4 tbsp water

fresh coconut meat from ½
    coconut (page 13), chopped

liquid from fresh coconut (page
    13)

16-oz can pigeon peas, drained

1 fresh chili pepper

1 tsp salt

freshly ground black pepper

2 tbsp vegetable oil

2 tbsp sugar

3½ lb chicken, chopped

1 cup uncooked rice, rinsed and
    drained

1¼ cups water

Put the onion, garlic, chives, thyme, celery, and 4 tablespoons water in a blender or food processor and process together. Empty the mixture into a large saucepan.

Make coconut milk using the coconut meat and liquid, following the directions on page 14.

Add the coconut milk to the pan with the pigeon peas and chili pepper. Cook over low heat for 15 minutes, then season with salt and freshly ground black pepper.

Heat the oil in a flameproof casserole. Add the sugar and heat until it begins to caramelize.

Add the raw chicken to the casserole and cook for 15 minutes until it has browned. Stir in the pigeon pea mixture, rice, and water. Bring to the boil, then reduce the heat, cover, and simmer for 20 minutes, or until the rice and chicken are cooked. Discard the chili pepper before serving.

Meat Dishes

ROAST PORK CALYPSO

BAKED PAPAYA WITH MEAT FILLING

PORK CHOPS PIÑA

CURRIED MEATBALLS

RABBIT IN PIMENTO SAUCE

SIRLOIN STEAK WITH PINEAPPLE CHUTNEY

STEWED LAMB SINT MAARTEN

LAMB AND SALT BEEF STEW

CURRIED LAMB WITH LENTILS

GOAT CURRY

ROAST PORK, PUERTO RICAN STYLE

PORKBURGERS WITH PINEAPPLE

CRISPED PORK CHUNKS WITH HOT PEPPER SAUCES

PORK CREOLE

STEAKS WITH ONIONS

CITRUSY PORK TENDERLOIN WITH MANGO-PAPAYA CHUTNEY

GINGER- AND RUM-GLAZED HAM

QUICK JERK PORK CHOPS

GINGERY PORK CHOPS WITH CURRIED MANGO

PIQUANT PORK CHOPS WITH AVOCADO SAUCE

JERK BURGERS

BEEF WITH BEANSPROUTS

BRAISED LAMB, PUERTO RICAN STYLE

ROAST PORK CALYPSO

SERVES 6

4-lb piece of pork
2 cups cold water
1 tbsp vinegar
1 tbsp salt
3 garlic cloves, crushed

1 tsp thyme
1 onion, grated
1 tsp ground cloves
1 tbsp chopped fresh parsley

Place the pork in a large saucepan and cover with the cold water. Add the vinegar, salt, garlic, and thyme and leave to marinate for several hours.

Meanwhile, mix the onion, cloves, and parsley together in a bowl.

Preheat the oven to 325°F.

After the pork has marinated, remove it from the saucepan and make 2-inch long gashes all over. Fill the holes with the onion mixture. Pour the marinade into a baking dish.

Lay the pork in the dish and roast in the preheated oven for 30 minutes, or until it is cooked through.

BAKED PAPAYA WITH MEAT FILLING

SERVES 6

2 tbsp vegetable oil
1 small onion, finely chopped
1 garlic clove, crushed
1 lb lean ground beef or lamb
4 ripe tomatoes, skinned and
    chopped
2 chilies for a hot dish, or ½
    thinly chopped fresh hot
    pepper for a mild flavor

1 tsp salt
freshly ground black pepper
5 lb green papayas, halved and
    deseeded
½ cup grated cheese

Preheat the oven to 350°F.

Heat the oil in a large skillet. Add the onion and garlic and fry for 5 minutes, then stir in the beef or lamb and continue frying until browned.

Add the tomatoes, chilies or hot pepper, salt, and freshly ground black pepper to taste. Continue to cook, stirring frequently, until all the liquid has evaporated.

Spoon the meat mixture into the papaya shells, and place them in a shallow roasting pan. Pour in enough boiling water around them to reach approximately 1 inch up the sides of the shells when they are placed side by side. Bake in the preheated oven for 1 hour.

Sprinkle with half the grated cheese and continue baking for 30 minutes longer. Serve sprinkled with the remaining grated cheese.

PORK CHOPS PIÑA

SERVES 4

½ cup pineapple juice

¼ cup dry white wine

1½ tbsp olive oil

¼ tsp salt

⅛ tsp freshly ground black
pepper

4 x 3-oz boneless pork chops

⅓ cup chopped onion

½ small chili pepper, seeded and
finely chopped

3 tomatoes, skinned, seeded,
and chopped

2 tbsp chopped fresh coriander

¼ tsp ground cinnamon

¼ tsp grated nutmeg

To prepare the marinade, combine the pineapple juice, wine, half the oil, salt and black pepper in a very large, sealable plastic food storage bag. Add the pork chops, seal the bag, squeezing out the air, and turn to coat the chops. Refrigerate for at least 2 hours or overnight, turning the bag over occasionally.

To prepare the sauce, heat the remaining oil in a small saucepan. Add the onion and pepper and cook, stirring frequently, for 5 minutes until tender. Add the remaining ingredients and simmer for 3 minutes longer.

Drain the marinade into the sauce, then bring to a boil and simmer for 10 minutes longer.

Meanwhile, broil the chops for 7 minutes on each side until cooked through but still juicy. Serve each chop with an equal amount of the sauce.

CURRIED MEATBALLS

MAKES 12

The Indian influence is more apparent in the cuisine of Jamaica, Trinidad, Guyana, and Surinam than it is in the cuisines of the other islands. Curry has become an integral part of Caribbean cooking. As a matter of fact, the national party dish of Jamaica is curried goat and rice. Rice and chicken curry or goat curry must be on the menu at every party! In Trinidad, pelau is the national dish. It is a beautiful saffron-colored rice dish with meat or seafood that is garnished with raisins and tomatoes.

Melt the butter or margarine in a medium-sized saucepan. Add the chopped onion and fry it for 1 to 2 minutes, then add the beef, salt, lemon juice, chili powder, and coriander. Remove the pan from the heat and shape the beef mixture into balls.

Heat the oil in the pan and add the grated onion, garlic, cloves, turmeric, sugar, and tomatoes. Simmer for 15 minutes, stirring frequently.

Add the meatballs and continue to cook for 15 minutes longer. Serve hot with steamed rice.

1 tbsp butter or margarine	*1 tbsp vegetable oil*
1 onion, chopped	*1 onion, grated*
1 lb lean ground beef	*1 garlic clove, crushed*
2 tsp salt	*pinch of ground cloves*
1 tsp lemon juice	*1 tsp turmeric*
1 tsp chili powder	*1 tsp sugar*
1 tsp ground coriander	*4 tomatoes, chopped*

RABBIT IN PIMENTO SAUCE

SERVES 4

2-lb rabbit, chopped into 2-in
  pieces
1 tsp salt
freshly ground black pepper
¼ cup butter or margarine
1 onion, chopped
1 fat garlic clove, chopped
2 tbsp brandy
2 tbsp dry sherry
3 ripe tomatoes, skinned and

  chopped
½ fresh chili pepper, chopped
⅓ cup drained canned pimentos,
  finely chopped
⅔ cup chicken stock
1 bay leaf
½ tsp sugar

Preheat the oven to 350°F.

Season the rabbit pieces with the salt and freshly ground black pepper to taste. Melt the butter or margarine in a large flameproof casserole dish and brown the rabbit on all sides. Transfer the rabbit to a dish and put to one side.

Add the onions and garlic to the casserole, cook them for 5 minutes, then pour them over the rabbit.

Pour the brandy into the casserole and heat it. Remove the casserole from the heat and set light to the brandy with a match. Shake the casserole backward and forward until the flame dies. Add the sherry to the brandy in the casserole and bring to a boil.

Add the tomatoes, chili pepper, pimentos, chicken stock, bay leaf and sugar, then season to taste with freshly ground black pepper. Add the rabbit and bring to a boil, then simmer for 30 minutes.

Remove the casserole from the heat, cover, and bake in the preheated oven for 2 hours. Serve with rice.

SIRLOIN STEAK WITH PINEAPPLE CHUTNEY

SERVES 4 TO 6

2 to 2¼ lb sirloin steak, cut 1½ in
  thick and trimmed of fat
3 tbsp vegetable oil
½ tsp salt
¼ tsp freshly ground black
  pepper
1 tsp curry powder
¼ tsp garlic powder
¼ tsp ground ginger
½ tsp ground allspice
dash of grated nutmeg
dash of ground cinnamon

FOR THE PINEAPPLE CHUTNEY

20-oz can crushed pineapple,
  drained
1 large scallion, finely chopped,
  including some green top
2 tbsp flaked coconut,
  preferably unsweetened
1/3 cup very finely chopped red
  bell pepper
1 tbsp hot pepper sauce
1 tbsp grated fresh gingerroot
1 tbsp fresh lime juice
1 tbsp dark rum
salt and freshly ground white
  pepper

Brush both sides of the steak with vegetable oil. Mix together the salt, pepper, curry powder, garlic, ginger, allspice, nutmeg, and cinnamon. Transfer the mixture to a large sheet of waxed paper and roll both sides of the steak in it, patting the mixture into the surface; set aside.

To make the chutney, combine the pineapple, scallion, coconut, red pepper, hot pepper sauce, ginger, lime juice, rum and salt and pepper in a glass bowl and toss gently. Cover and leave to stand at room temperature until ready to serve.

To cook the steak, place a large, heavy-bottomed skillet over medium-high heat. Add the remaining oil. When hot, add the steak and cook for 4 minutes on each side, or to taste. Alternatively, to barbecue: brush the grill rack with vegetable oil and place 5 to 6 inches from the coals. Grill the steak over glowing coals for about 8 minutes on each side for medium rare steaks. Transfer to a serving dish and serve with the chutney.

LAMB AND SALT BEEF STEW

SERVES 6

½ lb lean salt beef

¼ cup butter or margarine

1 tbsp vegetable oil

2 lb boned lamb or goat, cut
  into 1-in pieces

2 onions, finely chopped

1 large tomato, skinned and
  chopped

2 tsp chopped fresh gingerroot

¼ green bell pepper, cored,
  seeded, and chopped

1 fat garlic clove, chopped

½ fresh chili pepper, chopped

1 tsp salt

2 tsp ground cumin

2 tbsp lime or lemon juice

2½ cups water

3 potatoes, peeled and diced

2 cucumbers, peeled and diced

Put the salt beef in a saucepan, cover with cold water, and bring to a boil, then boil for 30 minutes. Drain the meat and cut it into cubes.

Melt the butter or margarine and oil in a large saucepan. Add the lamb or goat and brown it all over, then remove the meat and set to one side.

Add the onions to the saucepan and cook for 5 minutes. Then add the tomato, ginger, green pepper, garlic, chili pepper, salt, and cumin and cook for 10 minutes, stirring constantly.

Stir in the prepared salt beef, lamb, lime or lemon juice, and 2½ cups of water and continue cooking for 1 hour over low heat. Add the potatoes and cucumber and simmer for 20 minutes longer.

STEWED LAMB SINT MAARTEN

SERVES 4 TO 6

Traditionally, this dish from the Netherlands Antilles is made with goat. This lamb version, however, is equally delicious.

2 tbsp vegetable oil

2 lb boneless lamb, cut into 2-in cubes

2 onions, chopped

4 cloves garlic, chopped

½ cup chopped celery

1 tsp finely chopped fresh gingerroot

3 tbsp minced chili peppers

1 small green bell pepper, cored, seeded, and chopped

2 tomatoes, skinned and chopped

1 tbsp lime or lemon juice

1 tsp ground cumin

1 tsp ground allspice

2 cups beer

1 tbsp vinegar

½ cup chopped seeded cucumber

1 cup green pitted olives

4 tbsp drained capers (optional)

Heat the oil in a large saucepan over medium-high heat. Add the lamb and brown it in the oil, then remove from the pan and drain.

Add the onions, garlic, celery, ginger, chili peppers and green pepper and sauté until the onions are soft, stirring frequently.

Combine the lamb, onion mixture, tomatoes, lime or lemon juice, cumin, and allspice and cover with beer. Simmer for about 1½ hours until the meat is very tender and starts to fall apart; add more beer if necessary.

Add the vinegar, cucumber, olives, and capers, if using. Simmer for 15 minutes longer.

CURRIED LAMB WITH LENTILS

SERVES 6

2 tbsp oil

1 tbsp cumin seeds

1 tsp ground turmeric

1 large onion, chopped

2 garlic cloves, crushed

2-in piece of gingerroot, peeled
   and finely chopped

2 lb boned lamb or goat meat,
   cubed

1 chili pepper, chopped

1 cup lentils, rinsed and drained

14-oz can tomatoes, drained
   and chopped

1 tsp salt

freshly ground black pepper

2½ cups cold water

Heat the oil in a flameproof casserole. Add the cumin, turmeric, onion, garlic, and ginger and fry them for 5 minutes over medium heat. Add the lamb or goat meat and cook for 5 minutes longer.

Stir in the chili pepper, lentils, tomatoes, salt, and freshly ground black pepper to taste. Add the cold water, and bring to a boil, then lower the heat, cover, and simmer for 1 hour until the lamb or goat is tender and the sauce has become thick.

Serve with Roti or steamed rice and mango chutney.

GOAT CURRY

SERVES 6

3 lb goat meat, boned and
   chopped
1 tbsp salt
3 garlic cloves, crushed
1 tbsp vinegar or 2 tbsp lime or
   lemon juice
¼ cup vegetable oil

1 onion, sliced
½ tsp ground cumin
⅓ cup curry powder
1 large, fresh tomato, chopped
1 fresh chili pepper, sliced
pinch mint leaves, chopped, to
   garnish (optional)

Put the goat meat into a glass bowl with the salt, half the garlic, the vinegar or lime or lemon juice, and 2 tablespoons of cold water. Mix them together well and leave to marinate for 3 hours.

Heat the oil in a large saucepan over medium heat. Add the onion and remaining garlic and fry for 2 minutes until golden brown.

Mix the cumin and curry powder with a little water, add to the pan, and cook for 2 more minutes.

Add the meat and sauté for 5 minutes. Add the tomato and chili.

Bring to the boil, then lower the heat and simmer until the meat is tender. Garnish with chopped mint leaves. Serve with steamed rice.

Roast Pork, Puerto Rican Style

SERVES 8 TO 10

This is a favorite dish in Puerto Rico, where it is known as *Fabada Asturiana,* and the Puerto Rican love for assertive, spicy flavors is amply demonstrated in this recipe. Adjust the amount of onions and squash according to how many you wish to serve.

3 tbsp olive oil

1 tbsp minced garlic

½ tsp finely crumbled dried oregano leaves

¾ tsp ground cumin

1 tsp salt

½ tsp black pepper

4 large scallions, chopped

1 cup chopped fresh coriander

1 green bell pepper, cored, seeded and chopped

1 cup white rum

1 leg of pork (about 7 lb with bone)

2 x 8-oz baking potatoes, scrubbed, each cut lengthwise into 8 wedges

1 to 3 large red onions, each cut into 8

2 to 4 pieces squash, such as Hubbard or butternut, peeled and cut into 1-in slices (optional)

2 to 4 zucchini cut into 1-in slices (optional)

GRAVY

4 tbsp fat from drippings in roasting pan

¼ cup all-purpose flour

½ tsp black pepper

3½ cups water or beef stock

Heat the olive oil in a skillet. Add the garlic and fry until it is tender. Blend the olive oil-garlic mixture with the oregano, cumin, salt, pepper, scallion, coriander, green pepper, and rum to a paste in a blender or food processor.

Place the meat in a non-reactive baking pan slightly larger than the meat. With a long, sharp knife, score the top of the roast in a diamond pattern, cutting through the rind and underlying fat almost to the meat. Rub the seasoning paste into the roast, cover, and marinate in the refrigerator overnight.

Preheat the oven to 325°F.

Unwrap the meat and roast it for 2 hours. Add the potatoes, onions and squash, if using, to the roasting pan and brush with drippings, then roast for 1 hour longer.

Add the zucchini, if using, and brush with the drippings. Continue to roast for 45 minutes longer (the meat should roast for a total of 32 to 35 minutes per 1 lb), or until a meat thermometer inserted in the thickest part (not touching the bone) registers 185°F and the vegetables are tender.

Remove the meat to a chopping board and cover loosely with foil (reserve the pan drippings for gravy), then leave to stand for 15 minutes before slicing. Arrange the vegetables on a dish and cover to keep warm.

If you are planning to reserve some of the meat and pan juices for other meals, proceed as follows: slice one-third of the pork and serve with the vegetables, reserving 1 cup pan juices for gravy. Then slice half the remaining pork thinly (about 1 lb) and wrap tightly in heavy freezer bags. Shred the remaining meat (about 12 oz), cover and refrigerate; sliced pork will keep for 2 weeks in the freezer; shredded about 1 week in the refrigerator.

To make the gravy, pour the fat into a saucepan and sprinkle the flour into it. Beat over medium-high heat until smooth, scraping up browned bits on the bottom of the pan. Gradually whisk in the water or beef stock until blended. Bring to a boil, then reduce the heat and simmer for 5 minutes, or until thickened, stirring 2 or 3 times. Cool and refrigerate about half the gravy in a tightly sealed container if you are planning to use it for another meal.

PORKBURGERS WITH PINEAPPLE

SERVES 4

1 lb ground pork

1 tsp dried sage

4 scallions, chopped

1 cup fresh whole-wheat bread
    crumbs

salt and freshly ground black
    pepper

1 egg

1 tbsp sugar

2 tbsp cider or apple juice

4 slices fresh pineapple

Mix the pork with the sage, onions, bread crumbs, salt and
pepper, and egg. Knead the mixture so that it binds
together, then shape it into 4 burgers.

Heat a heavy-bottomed skillet and dry-fry the burgers
until they are brown on both sides and cooked through,
which will take 8 to 10 minutes. Transfer the burgers to a
heated serving dish.

Add the sugar, cider or apple juice to the juices in the
pan and heat through until the sugar dissolves. Bring to a
boil, then add the pineapple slices and continue cooking
until the pineapple is glazed in the juices.

Put a pineapple slice on top of each burger. Serve with
puréed potatoes and a green salad.

CRISPED PORK CHUNKS WITH HOT PEPPER SAUCES

SERVES 4 TO 6

The marinade renders the chunks tender inside, and browning them after simmering gives them a delicious crusty coating similar to meats grilled over an open fire.

3 lb pork tenderloin, cut into 1-in chunks

1 large onion, finely chopped

½ tsp dried thyme

1 cup orange juice; or ½ cup orange juice and ½ cup lime juice

1 fresh chili pepper, chopped

2 cloves garlic, minced

½ cup peanut oil

freshly ground black pepper to taste

salt to taste

¼ tsp ground cinnamon

½ tsp ground cumin

Mix the pork chunks with the onion, thyme, orange juice, hot pepper, garlic, pepper, and salt in a glass bowl. Cover and refrigerate for 6 to 8 hours.

Transfer meat to a large, heavy-bottomed skillet or saucepan and add cold water to cover the meat. Cook over medium heat until the liquid begins to boil, then reduce the heat and simmer for about 1 hour, or until the meat is cooked throughout.

Drain the meat and pat dry with paper towels. Heat the oil in a skillet and fry the meat quickly, turning each piece over as it is browned. Serve immediately with one or several of the sauces below:

PAPAYA HOT PEPPER SAUCE

MAKES ABOUT 2 CUPS

2 tbsp stemmed, seeded, and finely chopped chili peppers

½ cup chopped papaya

½ cup raisins

1 cup finely chopped onion

3 cloves garlic, minced

½ tsp turmeric

¼ cup distilled vinegar

Combine all the ingredients in a pan and bring to a boil, stirring constantly. Reduce the heat and cook for 5 minutes. Put the mixture in a blender and purée until smooth, then serve. Store in a tightly sealed glass jar.

HOT HOT HOT PEPPER SAUCE

MAKES ABOUT 2 CUPS

1 cup vinegar

7 tbsp lime or lemon juice

2 onions, finely chopped

6 radishes, finely chopped

2 cloves garlic, crushed

2 tbsp stemmed, seeded, and finely chopped chili pepper

4 tbsp olive oil

freshly ground black pepper and salt to taste

Combine all the ingredients in a glass bowl and serve. Store any leftover sauce in a tightly sealed glass jar.

LIME-HORSERADISH SAUCE

MAKES ABOUT 2 CUPS

3 tbsp grated horseradish

7 tbsp lime juice

7 tbsp mayonnaise

1/2 cup plain yogurt

salt and freshly ground black pepper

Blend all the ingredients in a blender or food processor, or in a glass mixing bowl, for 1 minute, until thoroughly combined. Chill (and store) in a tightly sealed glass jar overnight to allow flavors to blend completely.

PORK CREOLE

SERVES 4

1 tbsp any dry jerk seasoning
(page 19) or commercial jerk
seasoning

1½ to 2 lb pork tenderloin,
trimmed of fat
1½ cups chicken stock

Rub the seasoning all over the pork. Place the tenderloin on a plate, cover loosely with plastic wrap, and leave to marinate in the refrigerator for 2 to 3 hours.

Preheat the oven to 350°F.

Oil a large skillet and place it over high heat for about 3 minutes. Add the pork and sear on all sides, then transfer it to a baking dish and add the stock.

Roast, turning the meat occasionally and basting it with stock, for 25 to 30 minutes. The interior should be just pink. Cut into ½-inch slices and serve.

STEAKS WITH ONIONS

SERVES 6

6 very thin beef steaks
2 garlic cloves, crushed
2 tsp salt
freshly ground black pepper

1 tsp vinegar
¼ cup butter or margarine
1 onion, sliced
2 tsp brandy

Season the steaks with the garlic, salt, pepper, and vinegar, then leave them to stand for 3 hours.

Melt the butter or margarine in a large skillet. Fry the steaks quickly to brown them on both sides, then remove them to a warm plate.

Add the onion to the skillet and fry for 2 minutes.

Add the brandy to the pan and heat through. Pour the onion and brandy over the steaks and serve immediately with a green salad and baked sweet potatoes.

CITRUSY PORK TENDERLOIN WITH
MANGO-PAPAYA CHUTNEY

SERVES 4 TO 6

½ cup fresh orange juice

1 tbsp fresh lime juice

1½ tsp sugar

½ tsp salt

¼ tsp ground allspice

pinch of grated nutmeg

1 tsp grated fresh gingerroot

3 cloves garlic, minced

8 oz pork tenderloin

vegetable oil

½ tsp brown sugar

FOR THE MANGO-PAPAYA CHUTNEY

1 ripe mango; or 1 cup canned
   unsweetened mango cut into
   bite-sized chunks

1 ripe papaya; or 2 nectarines;
   or ¼ cup canned unsweetened
   papaya cut into bite-sized
   chunks

1 tbsp chopped scallion

1 tbsp fresh lime juice

1 tbsp chopped fresh coriander

1 tsp chopped chili pepper or
   hot pepper sauce

Combine the orange juice, lime juice, sugar, salt, allspice, nutmeg, ginger, and garlic in a large, sealable plastic food storage bag. Add the pork, seal the bag, and marinate in the refrigerator for 8 hours, turning the bag occasionally.

Preheat the oven to 350°F.

Remove the pork from the bag, reserving the marinade. Place the pork on a rack brushed with oil. Place the rack in a shallow roasting pan and pour hot water and half the reserved marinade into the roasting pan to a depth of ½ inch. Insert a meat thermometer into the thickest part of the pork and bake for 40 minutes, or until the meat thermometer registers 160°F, basting frequently with the remaining marinade mixed with brown sugar.

While the meat is cooking, combine the mango, papaya, scallion, lime juice, coriander and chili pepper or hot pepper sauce. Chill and serve with the pork.

GINGER- AND RUM-GLAZED HAM

SERVES 8 TO 10

7 to 8 lb half (shank end)
  smoked ham
2 tbsp grated fresh gingerroot
3 tbsp unrefined sugar

3 tbsp dark rum
coriander sprig to garnish
  (optional)

Preheat the oven to 350°F. If the ham still has the skin attached remove most of it with a sharp knife, leaving a layer of fat and a collar of skin around the bone. Trim the fat, leaving a layer about ¼ inch thick, and score the layer remaining into diamonds. Bake the ham on a rack in a roasting pan for 55 minutes.

Combine the ginger, sugar, and rum in a blender or food processor and blend together until smooth. Spread this glaze over the ham and bake for 30 to 35 minutes longer, or until the glaze is brown and bubbly.

Transfer the ham to a serving dish, garnish with coriander if desired, cover with foil, and leave to stand for 15 minutes before carving.

QUICK JERK PORK CHOPS

SERVES 4

If you marinate the chops overnight, next day throw them on the barbecue or under the broiler. The same rub can be used with lamb, chicken or rib steaks.

3 tbsp stemmed, seeded, and
  chopped chili peppers
3 tbsp ground allspice
3 tbsp lime juice
2 tbsp chopped scallion

1 tsp hot pepper sauce
1 tsp ground cinnamon
1 tsp grated nutmeg
4 pork chops

Purée the chili peppers, allspice, lime juice, scallion, hot pepper sauce, cinnamon, and nutmeg in a blender or food processor to make a thick paste.

Rub the mixture into the chops and marinate, covered, in the refrigerator for 1 hour or longer.

Broil the chops over a hot charcoal fire or under a hot broiler until cooked through and the juices run clear when pierced with the tip of a knife. The seasonings will cause the chops to char on the outside.

GINGERY PORK CHOPS WITH CURRIED MANGO

SERVES 6

6 pork chops, about 1 in thick,
  trimmed of fat
1½ tsp grated fresh gingerroot or
  ground ginger
3 cloves garlic, crushed
½ cup dry sherry or dry wine
½ cup ginger marmalade or
  orange marmalade
¼ cup soy sauce
2 tbsp light sesame oil

FOR THE CURRIED MANGO

2 mangoes, cut in bite-size
  chunks
2 tbsp butter or margarine,
  melted
¼ cup brown sugar
1 to 1½ tsp curry powder

Preheat the oven to 350°F. First make the curried mango. Place the drained mango in a pie dish. Combine the butter or margarine, sugar, and curry powder and spoon over the fruit. Bake in the oven for 30 minutes; keep warm until the pork chops are cooked.

With a knife point, make 6 incisions less than ½ inch deep on each side of the chops. Make a paste out of the ginger and garlic and rub it into the meat on both sides, spreading any remaining paste on top of the chops; set aside.

Combine the sherry or wine, marmalade, soy sauce and sesame oil. Mix together well and pour over the chops. Shortly before serving time, prepare the barbecue. Place a drip pan under the grill rack. Place the chops on the hottest part of the grill and cook, covered, for about 15 minutes, basting occasionally with the sauce and turning 2 or 3 times.

Alternatively, cook, uncovered, in the oven at 350°F.

PIQUANT PORK CHOPS
WITH AVOCADO SAUCE

SERVES 4

1 cup beer

¼ cup minced fresh basil

¼ cup fresh lime juice

2 tbsp plus ¼ tsp hot pepper
   sauce

1½ tsp dry mustard powder

½ tsp any dry jerk seasoning
   (page 19) or salt

2 cloves garlic, minced

4 x 5-oz lean pork chops, ½ in
   thick, trimmed of fat

2⅔ tbsp brown sugar

2 tbsp coarse-grain mustard

1 tbsp plus ¼ tsp cider vinegar

1½ tsp molasses

vegetable oil

FOR THE AVOCADO SAUCE

1 ripe avocado, peeled, seeded,
   and coarsely chopped

1 tbsp lime juice

¾ tsp chili powder

¼ tsp minced garlic

½ tsp salt

2 tbsp mayonnaise

Combine the beer, basil, lime juice, 2 tbsp hot pepper sauce, dry mustard powder, jerk seasoning or salt, and garlic in a large, sealable plastic food storage bag. Add the chops, seal the bag, and refrigerate for 8 hours, turning the bag occasionally.

Combine the brown sugar, mustard, vinegar, molasses, and remaining ¼ tsp hot pepper sauce in a small saucepan and bring to a boil. Reduce the heat immediately and simmer, uncovered, for 2 minutes; set aside.

Brush a grill rack with oil and place over medium-hot coals if barbecueing or under a medium-hot broiler. Remove the chops from the bag and discard the marinade. Place the chops on the rack and cook for 5 minutes. Turn the chops over and brush with brown-sugar mixture. Cook for 5 minutes longer, or until cooked through.

To make the avocado sauce, put the avocado, lime juice, chili powder, garlic, salt, and mayonnaise in a blender or food processor and purée until smooth. Serve the sauce with the chops.

A THRIVING SATURDAY MORNING MARKET WITH AN ABUNDANCE OF PRODUCE.

JERK BURGERS

SERVES 4

2 lb lean chuck steak, ground

½ tbsp any dry jerk seasoning
  (page 19) or prepared jerk
  seasoning

dash of hot pepper sauce

1 tsp sugar

1 small onion, chopped

1½ to 2 tbsp dry bread crumbs

vegetable oil

Blend the meat, jerk seasoning, hot pepper sauce, sugar, onion, and bread crumbs together in a large bowl.

Form the mixture into burgers. Cook them on a lightly oiled broiler rack or in a skillet, turning them once, until done.

If you like, sprinkle an extra coating of dry jerk seasoning on the burgers before you flip them over to make a charred crust. Serve on lightly toasted hamburger buns with lettuce and sliced onions and tomatoes.

BEEF WITH BEANSPROUTS

SERVES 4

1 lb lean beef, cut into tiny
   pieces
½ tsp salt
freshly ground black pepper
1 garlic clove, crushed

1 tbsp vegetable oil
1 tbsp soy sauce
1 onion, chopped
2 tbsp beef stock
½ cup fresh beansprouts

Season the beef with the salt, garlic, and freshly ground black pepper to taste.

Heat the oil in a skillet. Add the soy sauce and beef, then fry the beef until it is evenly browned. Add the onions and stock and cook for 5 minutes, stirring all the time. Lower the heat, add the beansprouts and cook for 10 minutes longer.

Serve with steamed rice and hot pepper sauce.

BRAISED LAMB, PUERTO RICAN STYLE

S E R V E S   6

6 lamb chops
3 tbsp honey
2 tbsp dry sherry
1/4 cup soy sauce
2 tbsp white-wine vinegar

2 garlic cloves, crushed
1/4 cup chicken stock
2 tsp brown sugar
2 tbsp dark rum

Place the lamb chops in a glass bowl. Mix all the remaining ingredients together and pour over the chops. Cover and refrigerate overnight.

The next day, preheat the oven to 350°F.

Put the chops and marinade in a baking dish and cover with foil or a lid. Bake for 45 minutes, then serve at once. Serve with baked cassava or breadfruit.

Side Dishes and Salsas

GREEN PLANTAIN CHIPS

STEWED OKRA

BLACK BEANS AND RICE

DEEP-FRIED STUFFED PLANTAIN RINGS

EGGPLANTS IN COCONUT SAUCE

EGGPLANT OR POTATO FRITTERS

SWEET POTATO AND WALNUT "SOUFFLE"

CHRISTOPHENE AND CARROTS

PLANTAIN AND APPLE PATTIES

SPLIT PEA FRITTERS

STUFFED GREEN BELL PEPPERS

BAKED CHRISTOPHENE

HOPPIN' JOHN

SWEETER-THAN-SWEET SWEET POTATOES

PAIN PATATE

CALYPSO RICE

JUG JUG

FRIED SWEET POTATOES

COCO-LOCO BEANS 'N' RICE

YUCA-CHIVE PANCAKES

PIGEON PEAS AND RICE

MANGO AND GREEN TOMATO CHUTNEY

PAPAYA-MANGO SALSA

BROILED TOMATO SALSA

PINEAPPLE SALSA

PINEAPPLE-COCONUT SALSA

SHRIMP SALSA

STAR FRUIT AND BLACK BEAN SALSA

GREEN PLANTAIN CHIPS

SERVES 6

4 green plantains

juice of ½ lime

salt

vegetable oil for deep frying

Peel the plantains (page 16) and rub them with the lime juice. Cut them into thin slices and mix well with a pinch of salt.

Heat some oil in a large skillet. Drain the plantain slices, then fry them for 3 minutes until they are crisp and golden brown. Remove them from the pan as soon as they are ready and drain them on paper towels. Serve when cool.

THIS TRADITIONAL JAMAICAN DISH IS DELICIOUS SERVED AS AN APPETIZER.

STEWED OKRA

SERVES 6

2 lb fresh okra

2 tbsp butter or margarine

1 medium to large onion, finely chopped

1 garlic clove, crushed

8 ripe tomatoes, skinned and chopped

½ chili pepper, chopped

1 tsp salt

Rinse the okra under cold running water. Cut ½ inch off the stalk, at the narrow end.

Melt the butter or margarine in a large saucepan over medium heat. Add the onions and garlic and fry until they are soft. Add the tomatoes and hot pepper and cook for 5 minutes longer.

Add the okra and salt and stir. Reduce the heat and cook for 20 more minutes, or until the okra are soft. Serve with rice and fried fish.

BLACK BEANS AND RICE

SERVES 6

When Cubans serve black beans and rice together, they call it *Moros y Cristianos*—Moors and Christians—after the Saracens who invaded Christian Spain in the 8th century A.D.

1¼ cups dried black beans

3 quarts water

3 tbsp vegetable oil

1 small onion, chopped

1 garlic clove, chopped

½ green bell pepper, cured, seeded and chopped

1¼ cups uncooked long-grain white rice

1 tsp salt

freshly ground black pepper

Rinse the beans in a colander under cold running water until the water runs clear.

Bring 2½ quarts of the water to a boil in a large saucepan. Add the beans, reduce the heat, and simmer for approximately 3 hours, or until the beans are tender.

Drain the beans in a colander. Mash 2 tablespoons of the beans to a smooth paste with a fork.

Heat the oil in a large skillet. Add the onion, garlic, and green pepper and cook them until soft.

Stir in the bean paste, and then add the rest of the beans. Reduce the heat and simmer, uncovered, for 10 minutes.

Return the contents of the skillet to the large saucepan. Add the rice, salt and remaining water and bring to a boil. Reduce the heat, cover, and simmer for 20 minutes, or until the rice is tender.

Season to taste with salt and freshly ground black pepper and serve immediately.

DEEP-FRIED STUFFED PLANTAIN RINGS

SERVES 4

2 big, ripe plantains

¼ cup butter or margarine

2 tsp vegetable oil

2 tbsp vegetable oil mixed with
   1 tsp liquid annatto

1 lb lean ground beef

1 small onion, chopped

½ green bell pepper, cored,
   seeded and chopped

1 fresh chili pepper, chopped

1 garlic clove, crushed

1 heaped tbsp all-purpose flour

3 ripe tomatoes, skinned and
   chopped

3 tbsp water

1 tsp salt

freshly ground black pepper

1½ tbsp vinegar

4 eggs

vegetable oil for frying

Peel the plantains (page 16).

Heat the butter or margarine with the vegetable oil in a large skillet. Cut each plantain lengthwise into 4 thick slices. Cook them in the pan for 4 minutes, turning them over now and again until they have browned. Drain them well on paper towels.

Heat the annatto-flavored oil in the same pan over medium heat. Add the beef, onion, green pepper, chili pepper, and garlic and cook for 5 minutes.

Add the flour and stir it in, then add the tomatoes, water, salt, and freshly ground black pepper to taste. Continue cooking until the mixture thickens. Stir in the vinegar.

Carefully bend each plantain slice around into a ring about 3 inches in diameter, securing the overlapping ends with a wooden toothpick. Lay the rings side by side.

Spoon the beef mixture into each ring, and press the tops as flat as possible.

Beat the eggs and brush some over the plantains.

Heat enough oil in a large pan to deep-fry the stuffed plantain rings. Fry them for about 3 minutes each side, turning them over very gently. Drain them well on paper towels, and serve as soon as they are all cooked.

EGGPLANTS IN COCONUT SAUCE

SERVES 6

2 lb eggplants

1 tbsp salt

8 tbsp oil

2 onions, sliced

2 garlic cloves, crushed

6 tomatoes, skinned and
  chopped

1¼ cups coconut milk (page 14)

freshly ground black pepper

2 tbsp shredded coconut

Cut the eggplants into ½-inch thic slices. Place them in a colander, sprinkling a little salt over each layer of slices, and leave, weighted down with a plate, for 20 minutes. Rinse off the bitter juices that will have oozed out, and dry with paper towels.

Heat 6 tablespoons oil in a large skillet. Fry the eggplant slices for 10 minutes, turning them once during this time. Drain them well on paper towels.

Preheat the oven to 350°F.

Heat the remaining oil in the same pan. Add the onions and fry for 5 minutes over medium heat. Add the garlic and tomatoes and cook for 3 minutes longer, stirring constantly.

Pour in the coconut milk and season to taste with salt and freshly ground black pepper. Layer the eggplant slices in a baking dish, then pour the coconut sauce over them. Cover with foil and bake for 30 minutes.

Uncover, sprinkle with the shredded coconut, and bake for 5 minutes longer.

EGGPLANT OR POTATO FRITTERS

SERVES 6

2 lb eggplants or potatoes
1 tbsp salt
generous ¾ cup all-purpose flour
freshly ground black pepper

4 scallions, chopped
½ chili pepper, chopped
½ cup cold water
vegetable oil for frying

Cut the eggplants into ½-inch thick slices and layer in a colander, sprinkling a little of the salt over each layer, then leave, weighted down with a plate, for 20 minutes. Rinse off the bitter juices and pat dry with paper towels. If using potatoes instead, simply slice thinly.

Put the flour, black pepper, scallions, chili pepper, and a pinch of salt into a large bowl and mix together well.

Gradually add the water to the bowl to make a smooth batter. Leave to rest for 10 minutes.

Heat enough oil in a large skillet to deep-fry the eggplant or potato slices.

Dip the eggplant or potato slices in the batter, then deep-fry them until they are golden brown. Place on paper towels to drain, then serve hot. Serve with a tomato or coconut chutney, if you like.

SWEET POTATO AND WALNUT "SOUFFLÉ"

SERVES 6

4 small sweet potatoes
2 tbsp butter or margarine
2 tbsp all-purpose flour
1 cup milk
½ small onion, grated

¼ tsp thyme
freshly ground black pepper
4 eggs, separated
1¼ cups chopped walnuts

Cook the sweet potatoes in boiling water until they are soft. Drain them and leave them to cool. Peel the sweet potatoes, then mash them with a fork.

Preheat the oven to its lowest setting. Grease a soufflé dish.

In a saucepan, melt the butter or margarine, then stir in the flour. Gradually add the milk, stirring, and cook until the sauce thickens.

Remove the pan from the heat and add the onion, thyme, and freshly ground black pepper. Beat the egg whites until stiff, then gently fold them into the sauce.

Add the walnuts and sweet potato, stirring them in gently. Beat the egg yolks and add these to the mixture. Pour the mixture into the greased soufflé dish. Bake in the preheated oven for 20 minutes, then serve immediately.

CHRISTOPHENE AND CARROTS

SERVES 4

½ cup water
1 tsp sugar
½ chicken stock cube
3 carrots, peeled and cut into
    ½-in slices
3 christophenes, peeled, seeded,
    and cut into 1-in chunks

2 tbsp butter or margarine
salt and freshly ground black
    pepper
1 tbsp chopped fresh parsley for
    garnish (optional)

Combine water, sugar, and stock cube in a large saucepan. Add the carrots and bring to a boil, then reduce heat and simmer for about 25 minutes. About 5 minutes before the carrots are cooked, add the christophenes and continue simmering until both are tender.

Melt the butter in a large skillet. Add drained vegetables. Stir to coat with butter and season with salt and pepper to taste. Garnish, if desired, and serve.

PLANTAIN AND APPLE PATTIES

SERVES 4

Apples, which can't be grown in the tropics, are not traditional to Caribbean cuisine, but they are sought after delicacies, especially on holidays. Combining "exotic" apples with plantains, this inspired dish can be festooned with crumbled streaky bacon, and complements ham and pork dishes.

2 ripe black plantains, peeled
  and grated
2 tart cooking apples, pared,
  cored, and grated
1 onion, chopped
2 tsp ground cinnamon
2 large gloves garlic, crushed

1 egg white
salt and freshly ground black
  pepper
1 tbsp butter or margarine
1 tbsp vegetable oil
1 slice bacon, fried, drained, and
  crumbled for garnish

Thoroughly mix together grated plantains and apples. Add the onion, cinnamon, garlic, egg white, salt and pepper.

Heat the butter and oil in a large skillet. Add large tablespoonfuls of the batter into pan and sauté until they are golden.

Turn the patties over and brown the other side. Drain well on paper towels before serving.

SPLIT PEA FRITTERS

MAKES 50

2 cups split pea flour
2 cups all-purpose flour
1 tsp baking powder
½ tsp turmeric

½ tsp salt
½ cup cold water
vegetable oil for frying

Mix the split pea flour, all-purpose flour, baking powder, turmeric, and salt together in a large bowl.

Add the water gradually, mixing well, to form a smooth batter.

Heat enough oil in a large skillet to deep-fry the fritters.

Drop spoonfuls of the batter into the oil and fry for 5 minutes until they are golden brown. Remove the fritters from the pan and leave them to drain on paper towels. Serve either hot or cool.

STUFFED GREEN BELL PEPPERS

SERVES 4

4 green bell peppers

2 cups cooked white rice

8 oz cooked shrimp, cleaned and
    cut into bite-sized pieces

1 cup Broiled Tomato Salsa
    (page 138)

1 cup sour cream

¼ cup chopped scallions

½ tsp ground cumin

1 tsp salt (optional)

Preheat the oven to 350°F. Lightly oil a 9- x 9-inch shallow baking dish.

Cut the tops off the bell peppers and reserve. Wash the peppers and remove the seeds and membranes.

Bring a large saucepan of water to a boil, then add the peppers and boil for 2 minutes. Remove the peppers from the water and drain well on paper towels.

Make the stuffing by combining all the remaining ingredients, adding the salt, if the rice was cooked without salt.

Gently spoon the stuffing into the peppers, then stand them in the baking dish. Put the tops back on the peppers and bake for about 40 minutes, until they are tender but not collapsing.

BAKED CHRISTOPHENE

SERVES 4

2 christophenes
1 cup water
½ tsp salt
1 onion, chopped

1 tbsp butter or margarine
freshly ground black pepper
1 tsp fresh bread crumbs

Preheat the oven to 350°F.

Peel the christophenes, then cut them into small pieces and boil in the water, to which the salt has been added, until soft. Drain well, and purée with a fork.

Add the onion, half the butter or margarine, and freshly ground black pepper.

Grease a baking dish with the remaining butter or margarine. Pour the puréed christophene into it, sprinkle with the bread crumbs, and bake in the preheated oven for 15 minutes.

HOPPIN' JOHN

SERVES 4

This dish is undoubtedly African in origin. No one quite knows how it got its name, but each cook seems to have his or her own recipe for this mixture of rice and black-eyed peas. Folklore holds that eating it on New Year's Day brings good luck, probably because the dish is so filling you won't want for much more.

3 cups water

2 chicken stock cubes

1 tomato, chopped

10 scallions, chopped

1 bay leaf

1 tsp dried thyme

1 tsp hot pepper sauce

1½ cups long-grain white rice

16-oz can black-eyed peas,
   drained and rinsed

1½ cups cooked ham trimmed of
   fat and cut in bite-sized cubes

salt and freshly ground black
   pepper

Put the water, stock cubes, tomato, scallions, bay leaf, thyme, and hot pepper sauce in a large saucepan and bring to a boil.

Add the rice, cover, and simmer for about 25 minutes until tender.

Stir in the black-eyed peas and ham, cover, and simmer for 8 to 10 minutes longer.

SWEETER-THAN-SWEET SWEET POTATOES

SERVES 4

Bring a taste of the tropics to your table in no time with this simple dish. It's wonderful with ham or pork chops, and with its bright color it doesn't need a garnish.

4 large sweet potatoes, boiled
  and sliced

2 x 8-oz can crushed pineapple,
  drained

½ tsp grated nutmeg

2 tsp grated fresh gingerroot

2 tsp ground cinnamon

2 tbsp dark rum

Preheat the oven to 350°F.

Layer the sweet potatoes in a baking dish. Combine the pineapple, nutmeg, ginger, cinnamon, and rum, then pour it over the potatoes.

Bake for 5 minutes and serve.

A SIMPLE SIDE DISH WHICH LOOKS AND TASTES WONDERFUL.

PAIN PATATE

SERVES 4

This aromatic Haitian dish is a sweet potato pudding using boniatos, the white-fleshed tropical tuber with a scent like that of violets. If you cannot find boniatos in your area, substitute ordinary white potatoes and add 1 teaspoon ground allspice to the dish.

10 oz boniato, grated

12-oz can evaporated milk

1 cup coconut milk (page 14)

3 very ripe bananas, puréed

¼ cup unrefined sugar

1 egg

½ teaspoon ground cinnamon

½ tsp grated nutmeg

1 tsp vanilla extract\

½ tbsp dark rum

2 tbsp unsalted butter, melted

grated peel of ½ lime

Preheat the oven to 400°F.

Mix together the boniato and evaporated milk, coconut milk, bananas, sugar, egg, spices, rum, butter, and lime peel.

Pour into a buttered baking dish and bake for about 1 hour. Serve warm or cool.

CALYPSO RICE

SERVES 4

1 cup long-grain white rice

1 tsp salt

2 oz baby corn

1 cup coarsely chopped
　mushrooms

¼ cup coarsely chopped water
　chestnuts

1 carrot, coarsely chopped

1 tbsp coarsely chopped fresh
　coriander or parsley

1 onion, coarsely chopped

½ red bell pepper, cored, seeded
　and coarsely chopped

½ green bell pepper, cored,
　seeded and coarsely chopped

4 tbsp butter or margarine

1½ tsp soy sauce

½ chicken breast (4 oz), cooked
　and coarsely chopped

¼ cup frozen green peas

Preheat the oven to 325°F.

Boil the rice in salted water until tender but still firm. Drain and set aside in a deep pan.

Melt the butter or margarine in a large saucepan. Add the baby corn, mushrooms, water chestnuts, carrots, coriander or parsley, onion, and peppers and sauté until they are all tender; set aside.

Add the soy sauce and chicken to the warm rice. Stir in the vegetables, then transfer to a 1-quart casserole and bake for 15 to 20 minutes.

Cook the peas just before removing the casserole from the oven. Drain the liquid from the peas, mix into the casserole and serve.

JUG JUG

SERVES 8

½ lb lean salt beef

3 cups dried pigeon peas

½ lb lean salt pork, cut into 5
　pieces

7½ cups water

¼ cup yellow cornmeal

1 tsp thyme

⅓ cup butter or margarine

1 onion, chopped

salt and freshly ground black
　pepper

Put the salt beef into a heavy saucepan with enough water to cover. Bring to a boil, then reduce the heat and simmer, covered, for about 3 hours.

Drain the beef, then chop it coarsely.

Wash the pigeon peas under cold running water, then put them, the salt pork, and water into a large saucepan. Bring to a boil, then reduce the heat, partially cover the pan and simmer for 2 hours.

Drain, reserving the cooking liquid; you should have just over 3 cups, but if it is less make it up to this amount with cold water. Chop the pork and peas coarsely.

Return the cooking liquid to the pan and bring to a boil, then pour in the cornmeal and beat it in. Add the thyme and boil for 10 minutes until the mixture is thick.

Melt one-third of the butter or margarine in a large skillet. Add the onion and cook for 5 minutes, until soft.

Stir in the cornmeal-thickened sauce, pork and peas, and beef. Season to taste with salt and freshly ground black pepper, and simmer for 20 minutes longer. Stir in the remaining butter and serve at once.

FRIED SWEET POTATOES

Instead of hash browns, fry diced sweet potatoes with onions and bacon for a side dish that goes as well with eggs at breakfast as with pork chops at dinner.

2 large sweet potatoes

8 slices bacon

2 tbsp bacon fat or butter

1 cup chopped onion

½ cup cored, seeded, and finely chopped bell pepper

1 tsp salt

¼ tsp freshly ground black pepper

⅛ tsp cayenne pepper

Parboil sweet potatoes in boiling water for 15 minutes. Drain them well and peel, then cut them into slices ½ inch thick. Immerse the slices in a bowl of water to cool them.

Dice the potatoes. While the potatoes are cooling, cook the bacon. When it is crisp, crumble it.

Heat 2 tablespoons bacon fat or butter in a large skillet. Add the onion and green pepper and fry for 5 minutes. Add the diced sweet potatoes and seasonings. Continue frying, stirring occasionally, for 10 to 15 minutes until the potatoes are tender.

Add the bacon bits and cook for 1 minute longer.

COCO-LOCO BEANS 'N' RICE

SERVES 4

Jamaicans make a version of this colorful dish called Jamaican Coat of Arms. This adaptation, though, also borrows from Haitian cuisine with the addition of pungent mushrooms.

2 cups water
1½ oz dried Haitian black mushrooms or porcini, coarsely broken up and presoaked in hot water for 30 minutes (optional)
2 cups coconut milk (page 14)
8-oz can red kidney beans, rinsed
1 tsp distilled vinegar
1 tsp dried thyme
3 whole peppercorns, crushed

2 whole allspice berries, crushed
1 cup long-grain white rice
1 small onion, coarsely chopped
1 garlic clove, crushed
vegetable oil for frying
⅓ cup coarsely chopped cooked and drained bacon
1 tsp salt for cooking rice
salt and freshly ground black pepper to taste

Bring the water, mushrooms, and coconut milk to a boil in a large saucepan, skimming the surface.

Add the beans, vinegar, thyme, peppercorns, and allspice. Reduce the heat, cover, and simmer for 10 minutes. Stir in the rice with a fork. Reduce the heat to low, cover, and cook for about 20 minutes, or until the rice is tender.

In the meanwhile, heat a small amount of oil in a frying pan. Add the onion and garlic and fry until they are tender. Add to the rice-and-beans mixture, along with the chopped bacon.

Bring to a simmer, then cover and cook for 10 minutes. Fluff the mixture, with a fork, adding salt and pepper to taste, and serve.

AN ISLAND CAFE THAT SERVES LOCAL SPECIALTIES AND COOLING DRINKS.

YUCA-CHIVE PANCAKES

SERVES 4

The mild, oniony flavor of chives gives a needed flavor boost to this otherwise bland tuber. These make tasty accompaniments to most main dishes. Serve them with a dollop of Lime-Horseradish Sauce (page 109).

1 lb fresh yuca, peeled
2 tbsp snipped fresh chives
1 egg, beaten
salt and freshly ground black
  pepper
½ cup dry bread crumbs
6 tbsp butter

Boil the yuca for 35 to 45 minutes until it can be easily pierced with a fork; drain well. When cool enough to handle, remove any stringy sections and discard. Cut the yuca into 1-inch slices and purée in a blender or food processor. Press through a coarse strainer into a bowl and stir in the chives, egg, salt and pepper.

Form into 3-inch patties about ½ inch thick.

Place the bread crumbs in a small bowl. Turn each pattie in the bread crumbs to coat, shaking off excess.

Melt the butter in a heavy-bottomed skillet over medium-high heat. Add the patties and cook for 5 minutes on each side until they are golden brown. Remove from the frying pan with a pancake turner and drain on paper towels. Serve immediately.

PIGEON PEAS AND RICE

SERVES 4

This dish is eaten on many of the islands. In the Bahamas it's called, appropriately enough, Bahamian Pigeon Peas and Rice. In Puerto Rico, it's called *arroz con gandules*. If you can't find pigeon peas, substitute small red kidney beans. This dish is great with chicken or any meat and can make a one-dish meal if leftover bits of meat are added.

2 tbsp oil

1 small onion, chopped

2 cloves garlic, crushed

4 tbsp tomato paste

2 ripe tomatoes, chopped

1 green bell pepper, cored, seeded, and chopped

½ tsp dried thyme

4 tbsp chopped fresh coriander

16-oz can pigeon peas, drained

1 cup long-grain white rice

2 cups water

2 tbsp fresh lime juice

hot pepper sauce to taste

salt and freshly ground black pepper

Heat the oil in a saucepan. Add the onion and fry gently for 5 minutes. Add the garlic and tomato purée, chopped ripe tomatoes, green peppers, and thyme and continue frying for 1 minute longer.

Add the coriander, pigeon peas, and rice and fry, stirring frequently, for 1 minute.

Add the water and lime juice and cook gently, covered, for 15 minutes until the rice is tender. Add hot pepper sauce, salt and pepper to taste, and serve.

MANGO AND GREEN TOMATO CHUTNEY

MAKES ABOUT 4 LB

2 lb mangoes, peeled and
  quartered
1½ lb cooking apples, peeled and
  chopped
1 cup chopped onion
1 lb green tomatoes, chopped
1 cup raisins
juice of 1 large lemon

2½ cups vinegar
2 tbsp salt
¼ tsp cayenne pepper
¼ tsp grated nutmeg
3 bay leaves
1½ tbsp lime juice
5 cups unrefined sugar

Place all the ingredients, except the lime juice and sugar, in a large bowl, mix thoroughly, and leave to stand for at least 3 hours.

Transfer the mixture to a preserving pan and bring to the boil, then lower the heat and simmer gently until tender, stirring frequently.

Add the lime juice and sugar and stir until the sugar dissolves. Continue to simmer until the chutney thickens and is of the desired consistency. Pour into warmed jars, cover, and label.

PAPAYA-MANGO SALSA

MAKES ABOUT 2 CUPS

Complements swordfish, trout, blue fish, catfish, grilled or barbecued beef, barbecued shrimp and sliced cold roast beef.

½ papaya, peeled, seeded, and
  cut into bite-size cubes
½ mango, peeled and cut into
  bite-size cubes
1 fresh jalapeño pepper, seeded
  and minced

1 scallion, minced
1 tbsp sugar
1 tbsp chopped fresh coriander
1 tbsp finely chopped red bell
  pepper
papaya seeds to taste (optional)

Combine all ingredients in a glass bowl, then cover and refrigerate. Serve chilled.

MANGO AND GREEN TOMATO CHUTNEY —
A COMBINATION OF SWEET AND SHARP FLAVORS.

PINEAPPLE-COCONUT SALSA

MAKES ABOUT 1½ CUPS

PINEAPPLE SALSA

MAKES ABOUT 2 CUPS

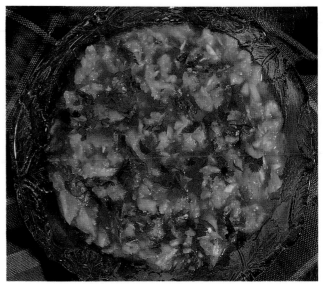

1 cup diced ripe pineapple

½ cup seeded and diced yellow
  bell pepper

1 small red onion, diced

7 tbsp diced chili pepper

6 heaped tbsp unsweetened
  shredded coconut

1 tbsp sherry vinegar

Combine all ingredients in a bowl. Cover and let stand at room temperature for 10 to 15 minutes before serving.

1 lb peeled and cored fresh ripe
  pineapple, or tinned crushed
  pineapple in own juice

3 tbsp chopped fresh coriander

2 tsp freshly squeezed lime juice

⅛ tsp ground cumin

⅛ tsp freshly ground white
  pepper

Combine all ingredients in a glass bowl. Cover and refrigerate. Serve chilled.

BROILED TOMATO SALSA

MAKES ABOUT 1½ CUPS

3 large tomatoes

½ cup finely chopped onion

2 cloves garlic, minced

2 chiles, seeded and minced

3 tbsp finely chopped fresh
  coriander

1 tbsp olive oil

1 tbsp fresh lime juice

salt to taste

Core the tomatoes. Then cut them in half and squeeze the seeds out. Place the tomatoes, cut side down, on a broiler-safe baking sheet and place them under the broiler. Broil the tomatoes until the skin is just slightly blackened and loose. Slide off their skins, drain off excess juice, and let them cool.

While the tomatoes are cooling, mix together all the remaining ingredients. Then chop the tomatoes and add them to the salsa. Let sit for 15 minutes or so, then taste and adjust the seasoning.

SHRIMP SALSA

MAKES ABOUT 2 CUPS

A cool, easy dip for crackers, chips, or vegetables. Make a couple hours in advance to let the flavors blend. Taste again just before serving and adjust the hot pepper sauce.

2 tomatoes, seeded and chopped

½ cucumber, peeled, seeded, and diced

3 scallions, finely chopped

1 mild chili pepper, seeded and finely chopped

2 tbsp chopped fresh cilantro

1½ tbsp cider vinegar

dash of salt

few drops of hot pepper sauce

4 oz tiny shrimp, cooked and shelled

Combine all ingredients together in a bowl. Cover and refrigerate for at least 2 hours before serving.

THIS SALSA WILL ENHANCE THE FLAVOR OF ANY FISH OR POULTRY DISH.

STAR FRUIT AND BLACK BEAN SALSA

MAKES ABOUT 4 CUPS

C omplements barbecued or grilled or broiled fish and poultry dishes.

one 8-oz can black beans, drained

¾ cup corn kernels, fresh, frozen, or canned, drained

1½ cups chopped tomatoes

4 scallions, chopped

½ green bell pepper, cored, seeded, and finely diced

½ red bell pepper, cored, seeded, and finely diced

2 tbsp vegetable oil

½ cup red-wine viengar

hot pepper sauce to taste

Worcestershire sauce to taste

ground cumin to taste

salt and freshly ground black pepper

1 star fruit, ½ sliced crosswise in thin sections, ½ diced

Mix the beans, corn, tomatoes, onions, peppers, oil, and vinegar together in a glass bowl. Season to taste with the hot-pepper sauce, Worcestershire sauce, cumin, and salt and pepper.

Stir the diced star fruit slices into the mixture and place the others across the top. Cover and refrigerate at least 3 hours to allow flavors to blend, then serve chilled.

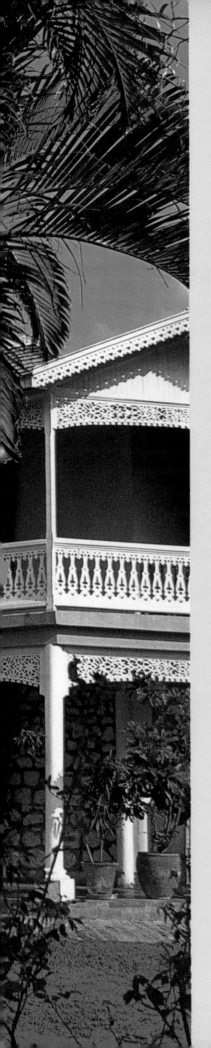

Tropical Desserts

MANGO MOUSSE

PUMPKIN PIE

TROPICAL DESSERT SALSA

BANANA FRITTERS

TROPICAL FRUIT SALAD

GUAVA FOOL

PAPAYA AND LIME ICE CREAM

SOURSOP ICE CREAM

TROPICAL FRUIT FOOL

EXOTIC PINEAPPLE

COCONUT CAKE

MANGO MOUSSE

SERVES 8

5 ripe mangoes	*pinch of salt*	
3 tbsp lime or lemon juice	*¼ cup sugar*	
2 egg whites	*6 tbsp heavy cream*	

Dice the flesh of 2 of the mangoes, and purée the rest in a blender or food processor.

Put the purée into a glass bowl and stir in the lime or lemon juice.

Beat the egg whites with the salt until they are frothy. Sprinkle in the sugar, and continue to beat until stiff. Gently fold in the cream.

Gradually stir the egg-white mixture into the mango purée. Spoon the diced mango over.

Spoon the mousse into serving bowls or glasses, and then chill for at least 3 hours before serving.

PUMPKIN PIE

SERVES 6

1 lb pumpkin	*½ tsp freshly grated nutmeg*
1 cup water	*1 tsp cinnamon*
1 tbsp butter or margarine	*⅓ cup sugar*
2 eggs	*store-bought 9-in piecrust,*
⅔ cup milk	*baked and cooled*

Peel the pumpkin and cut the flesh into cubes. Cook the flesh in the water until it is soft, then drain it and purée it with a fork.

Melt the butter or margarine in a saucepan over medium heat. Beat the eggs and mix in the milk, nutmeg, and cinnamon. Add this mixture to the melted butter or margarine and cook for 15 minutes, stirring frequently.

Preheat the oven to 450°F.

Pour in the sugar and puréed pumpkin, stir well together, and continue cooking for 10 minutes longer.

Remove the pan from the heat and leave the pie filling to cool.

Spoon the pumpkin filling into the piecrust and bake for 10 minutes, then lower the heat to 300°F and continue baking until firm.

TROPICAL DESSERT SALSA

MAKES ABOUT 3 CUPS

This is a sweet salsa, with a touch of spiciness from the chili powder. Adjust the amount of chili powder depending on how hot you want the salsa and whether you are using commercial chili powder or ground dried chilis. For variety, add a tablespoon of chopped fresh mint. Like the other dessert salsas, it is good over or in ice cream.

1 mango, peeled, pitted, and cut into ¼-in dice	*1 tbsp brown sugar*
1 cup cantaloupe, cut into ¼-in dice	*1 tsp chili powder, or to taste*
1 cup fresh pineapple, cut into ¼-in dice	*1 tbsp fresh orange juice*
	1 tbsp fresh lime juice

Combine all the ingredients in a glass bowl. Let sit for 30 minutes, then taste and adjust the seasonings. Cover and chill until required.

MAKE USE OF MANY OF THE
SUCCULENT FRUITS OF THE CARIBBEAN.

BANANA FRITTERS

SERVES 6

2 cups all-purpose flour

pinch of salt

1 tsp baking powder

½ cup milk

1 egg

1 tbsp butter or margarine,
   melted

⅓ cup sugar

3 small, ripe bananas

3 tbsp light rum

2 tbsp lime or lemon juice

vegetable oil for frying

½ cup grated coconut or cheese

Make a batter by putting the flour, salt, baking powder, milk, egg, melted butter or margarine, and a third of the sugar in a blender or food processor and mixing it at high speed. Pour the batter into a bowl.

Peel the bananas and cut them into 1-inch slices. Mix them in a bowl with the rum, lime or lemon juice, and half the remaining sugar. Leave them to marinate for 1 hour.

Heat the oil in a little skillet until it is very hot. Drain the banana slices, then dip them into the batter letting any of the excess drip off. Fry until they are golden brown, then drain them well on paper towels.

Sprinkle the grated coconut or grated cheese over the banana slices. Place them under a hot broiler for 2 minutes until golden brown. Serve hot.

TROPICAL FRUIT SALAD

SERVES 6

1 fresh pineapple, peeled and
   sliced, or 14-oz can pineapple
   slices, drained

3 tbsp rum

¼ cup brown sugar

juice of 1 lemon

2 bananas, sliced

2 mangoes, sliced

2 ripe guavas, sliced

5 tbsp grated fresh coconut

½ tsp freshly grated nutmeg

Put the pineapple slices into a glass bowl. Add the rum and sugar and chill, covered, for 1 hour.

Pour in the lemon juice, and mix in all the fruit. Serve sprinkled with the grated coconut and nutmeg.

THE SWEET, RICH TASTE OF RIPE BANANAS MAKE THIS A PARTICULARLY SATISFYING DESSERT.

PAPAYA AND LIME ICE CREAM

2 papayas (about 1¼ lb)
juice of 2 limes
2 tbsp fresh orange juice

1½ cups confectioners' sugar
1¼ cups heavy cream, whipped

Peel the papayas, then halve them and remove the pits. Purée the flesh and mix it with the juices and sugar.

Fold in the whipped cream and pour into a suitable container. Freeze until firm, beating twice at intervals.

Put in the refrigerator 30 minutes before serving. If liked, serve with extra pieces of papaya and a crisp cookie.

GUAVA FOOL

4 ripe guavas, trimmed and cut
into 1-in pieces

8–12 tsp confectioners' sugar
½ cup heavy cream

Purée guavas with half the sugar in a blender or food processor. Taste and add more sugar, if desired, and purée again. Repeat if necessary to add more sweetness.

Press the mixture through a strainer, cover, and chill.

Before serving, whip the cream and fold it into the purée in a swirling pattern.

THE SWEET TASTE OF PAPAYA AND TANGY LIME COMBINE PERFECTLY.

SOURSOP ICE CREAM

1 soursop
2 cups water
2 x 14-oz cans condensed milk
1¼ cups evaporated milk

1 tsp butter or margarine
¼ tsp vanilla extract
sugar to taste
3 tbsp cornstarch

Cut the soursop in half. Remove the flesh with a spoon and mix it with a quarter of the water. Press it through a nylon strainer to extract the pulp.

Put the milks and remaining water in a saucepan and bring to a boil. Add the butter or margarine, vanilla extract, and sugar to taste.

Mix the cornstarch with a little warm water, then add it to the mixture in the pan, stirring all the time until it thickens well. Remove the pan from the heat and leave the mixture to cool.

Add the soursop pulp to the pan, mix it in well, then transfer to shallow freezer containers and freeze for 3 hours, beating it every 30 minutes or so to break down the ice crystals. Otherwise, follow the instructions if you have an ice cream maker.

Remove the ice cream from the freezer at least 30 minutes before serving so it will be softened and easy to scoop. Serve in pretty sundae dishes.

TROPICAL FRUIT FOOL

SERVES 4

¾ lb fresh pineapple, papaya, or   ½ tsp vanilla extract
  mango, finely chopped   3 tbsp confectioners' sugar
1¼ cups heavy cream

Drain the pineapple, papaya, or mango.

Whip the cream with the vanilla extract and a third of the confectioners' sugar.

Chill the cream and pineapple, papaya, or mango separately for 1 hour.

Just before serving, fold the cream into the pineapple, papaya or mango, and serve at once in small bowls.

EXOTIC PINEAPPLE

SERVES 4

1 pineapple   3 passion fruit
3 tbsp kirsch   2 small bananas
1½ cups chopped dates   1 tbsp shredded coconut,
1 mango   toasted

Cut the top off the pineapple. Scoop out the flesh and remove the hard core. Place the pineapple flesh and kirsch in a bowl with the dates.

Slice the mango. Cut the passion fruit in half, scoop out the flesh and add with the mango to the pineapple.

Slice the bananas and add with the coconut. Mix the fruits together and return to the pineapple shell. If liked, serve slightly chilled with any extra fruit served separately.

THIS JAMAICAN DESSERT IS SIMPLY DELICIOUS.

COCONUT CAKE

SERVES 8 TO 12

A thick lemon custard is hidden between the layers of this white frosted cake.

2 cups all-purpose flour
1 tbsp baking powder
½ tsp salt
1½ cups sugar
½ cup butter
1 cup milk
1 tsp vanilla extract
1 cup shredded coconut
4 egg whites

2 tbsp fresh lemon juice
pinch of salt
6 tbsp heavy cream
1 tbsp butter

FOR THE FROSTING

1¼ cups sugar
¼ cup water
2 tbsp corn syrup
3 egg whites
¼ tsp cream of tartar
1 tsp vanilla extract
3 to 5 oz coconut, shredded

FOR THE LEMON FILLING

2 egg yolks
½ cup sugar
2 tsp finely grated lemon peel

Preheat oven to 350°F. Grease and flour two 9-inch round cake pans.

Sift together the flour, baking powder, and salt. Cream the butter with the sugar in a large bowl. Add the vanilla to the milk, then add it alternately with the flour to the butter-sugar mixture. Stir in the coconut.

In a separate bowl, beat the egg whites until stiff peaks form. Gently fold the whites into the batter.

Pour the batter into the cake pans. Bake for about 25 minutes, or until a knife inserted in the centers comes out clean. Let the layers cool completely before filling and icing them.

To make the lemon filling, combine all ingredients, except butter, in the top of a double saucepan, over simmering water. Stir constantly for 8 to 10 minutes until the custard thickens. Remove the pan from heat and beat in the butter. Let the custard cool.

Place the bottom layer of the cake on a platter, with the top side down. When the custard is cool, spread it on the bottom layer of the cake. Place the upper layer on top of the custard, right side up.

To make the frosting, combine all the ingredients, except the vanilla and coconut, in the top of a double saucepan, over rapidly boiling water. Beat them constantly with a hand-held beater for 7 minutes until the frosting holds soft peaks.

Remove the pan from the heat and beat in the vanilla. Continue beating, if necessary, until the frosting is right for spreading.

Spread the frosting across the top and down the sides of the cake. Sprinkle the coconut over the top and gently press it into the sides.

Island Drinks

PEANUT PUNCH

BANANA DAIQUIRI

PINA COLADA

JAMAICAN RUMBA

RUM DAISY

WATERMELON COOLER

MAWBY

GUAVA AND YOGURT REFRESHER

MANGO FRAPPÉ

GINGER BEER

PEANUT PUNCH

SERVES 4

⅓ cup smooth peanut butter or 1
   cup roasted peanuts, finely
   ground
14-oz can evaporated milk
14-oz can condensed milk
1 cup water
1 tbsp sugar (optional)

1 egg
pared peel of 1 lime or lemon
1 tsp vanilla extract
2 cups white rum or 1 cup milk
   (optional)

Mix the peanut butter or ground peanuts with the evaporated milk. Add the condensed milk and water, and mix together well. Taste and, if it is not sweet enough, add the sugar.

Beat the egg with the lime or lemon peel, then discard the peel.

Add the egg mixture, vanilla, and rum or milk to the peanut and milk mixture.

Bottle and chill. Serve with ice cubes.

BANANA DAIQUIRI

SERVES 4.

juice of ½ lime or lemon
1 tsp sugar
½ cup chopped banana, canned
   mango, or pineapple

¼ cup white rum
12 ice cubes, crushed
4 cherries to decorate

Blend all the ingredients, except the cherries, together with the ice.

Serve in cocktail glasses decorated with cherries on cocktail sticks.

PEANUT PUNCH IS A RICH AND SMOOTH DRINK.

PINA COLADA

SERVES 2

2 tbsp coconut cream

3 tbsp rum

⅓ cup unsweetened pineapple
   juice

⅔ cup crushed ice

2 slices pineapple to decorate

2 cherries to decorate

Blend all the ingredients, except the pineapple and cherries, together in a blender or food processor for 10 seconds.

   Serve in tall glasses with a straw, decorated with pineapple slices and cherries.

JAMAICAN RUMBA

SERVES 3 TO 4

2-in slice fresh pineapple, skin
    removed
¼ cup coconut milk (page 14)
4 tbsp white rum
1 small banana, peeled

2 tsp honey
1¼ cups milk
crushed ice to serve
sliced pineapple to decorate
sliced banana to decorate

Place all the ingredients, except the ice and garnishes, in a blender or food processor and process until smooth. Taste and add extra rum, if desired.

Serve chilled with crushed ice and decorate each glass with sliced banana and pineapple.

RUM DAISY

SERVES 2

2 tbsp white rum
juice of ½ lemon
1 tbsp grenadine syrup

2 cherries to decorate
2 slices banana to decorate

Mix all the liquid ingredients together. Decorate the glasses with cherries and banana slices.

WATERMELON COOLER

SERVES 4 TO 6

½ small watermelon   sugar to taste

Cut the watermelon into quarters and scoop out the flesh, removing the seeds.

Place the watermelon in a blender or food processor and process until smooth, adding a little sugar, which sweetens the flavor and strengthens the color.

Strain into a jug and chill well before serving.

MAWBY

SERVES 10

4 oz mawby bark   2 quarts cold water
3 bay leaves   white sugar to taste

Put the mawby bark, bay leaves, and cold water into a large saucepan. Bring to a boil, then lower the heat and simmer for 10 minutes. Remove the pan from the heat and leave it to stand until it has cooled completely.

Strain out the bark and bay leaves, and refrigerate the liquid in bottles for use as required.

To prepare the drink, combine the sugar and cold water, heat until the sugar dissolves and cool again.

Add some of the refrigerated mixture, and serve with ice cubes. If you want the drink less bitter, just add less of the mawby mixture to the syrup.

WATERMELON COOLER

GUAVA AND YOGURT REFRESHER

SERVES 4 TO 6

8 oz fresh guava
2½ cups plain yogurt
1¼ cups tonic water

2 tsp lemon or lime juice
sugar to taste
cucumber slices to decorate

Peel and quarter the guava and remove the coarse seeds in the center. Place it in a blender or food processor with the yogurt. Process, then pour into a jug.

Add the tonic water, lemon or lime juice, and sugar to taste. Serve well chilled. Decorate with cucumber.

MANGO FRAPPÉ

SERVES 3 TO 4

1 large ripe mango
5 ice cubes, crushed
2 tsp sugar

2½ cups sparkling Chardonnay
mango slices to decorate

Cut the flesh from the mango, save 3 or 4 thin slices for the decoration, then place the remaining flesh in a blender or food processor with the crushed ice and sugar. Process until smooth.

Strain into a serving jug, pour in the Chardonnay, stir, and serve at once. Decorate with the reserved mango slices.

GINGER BEER

SERVES 6

4-oz piece fresh gingerroot

juice of 1 lime or lemon

3 whole cloves

4 cups sugar

2½ quarts water

Peel the gingerroot and slice it thinly.

Put the ginger slices, lime or lemon juice, cloves, and sugar in the cold water in a saucepan. Bring to a boil and boil for 5 minutes.

Remove the pan from the heat and leave it to stand overnight.

The next day, strain and taste the drink. If it is not sweet enough, add more sugar; if it is too sweet, add more water. Bottle the ginger beer, adding a whole clove to each bottle. Cap the bottles and leave them to stand for 5 days. Chill and serve with ice cubes.

Index